LIVING
WHILE
DYING

LIVING
WHILE
DYING

*What to Do and What to
Say When You, or Someone
Close to You, is Dying*

DR R. GLYNN OWENS and FREDA NAYLOR

FOREWORD BY RABBI JULIA NEUBERGER

THORSONS PUBLISHING GROUP

First published 1989

306.9

British Library Cataloguing in Publication Data

Owens, R. Glynn
Living while dying
1. Death
I. Title   II. Naylor, Freda M.
306.9

ISBN 0-7225-1620-7

Published by Thorsons Publishers Limited, Wellingborough, Northamptonshire, NN8 2RQ, England

Printed in Great Britain by Billing & Sons Limited, Worcester

1 3 5 7 9 10 8 6 4 2

Contents

Dedication

This book is dedicated, with much love, to Les, Elizabeth, Madeleine and Phillipa, and to Lizzie.

Foreword
by Rabbi Julia
Neuberger

There can be few dying people as brave as Freda Naylor. When she was told that she had cancer she chronicled everything that was happening to her in order to make use of the experience for other people.

This is both a teaching book, in that it helps those who care for dying people professionally to see some of the effects of their totally well-meaning attempts to help, and a book of comfort for those who are going through the experience. Out of a deeply painful experience for herself and her family, she, with Glynn Owens, has fashioned a wise, witty and helpful record of all that took place.

We need the help too, for all too few of us, professional carers or families caught up in looking after one of their own who is dying, really know what to say. And even if we have a glimmering of an idea about that, it is still extraordinarily hard to bring ourselves to believe that honesty is what is needed. Freda, along with her co-author, Glynn Owens, makes it quite clear that the final truths, the last communications, have to be told with unswerving honesty because there is, all the time, a sense of heightened awarenesss that the day in question might be the last. Everything therefore has to be done properly, said properly, and enjoyed properly. It is a huge effort, and all help in achieving the desired result is enormously welcome.

This is, of course, only one woman's story, remarkable and moving though it is. It has to be admitted that people do vary in what they want to know and how they wish to be treated, but we can nevertheless extrapolate enough from this account to give us enormous help in caring for someone who is dying, or even in going through a terminal illness oneself.

It cannot have been an easy book to write. Neither author

suggests for one minute that this just flowed from the pen. But the very difficulty and pain within it make it all the more useful. It pulls no punches about what might be unpleasant. But it banishes fear by its honesty and clarity.

But it also serves another useful purpose. Few of us, having grown up in twentieth century Britain, have an intimate or personal experience of dealing with death as an everyday occurence. It has been made clinical, distant, and sanitized. What is so brilliant here is the removal of the protective sanitary wrapping from the subject, so that we can see it as it is and was for one remarkable woman, and come to accept and be able to work with an ordinary, though sad, domestic event in as calm and loving and peaceful way as possible.

1
The experience of dying

Almost half the male population and nearly a quarter of the female population will die before reaching the age of 70. By middle age, most people will have experienced the death of someone close to them — a parent or grandparent or, perhaps, a close friend or more distant relative. Only 10 per cent of these deaths will have been unexpected, mainly due to cardiovascular problems. The remaining 90 per cent will have involved some degree of expectation and preparation. Many people will die at home in the care of family and friends who know they are dying. For example, approximately half of the patients who die of cancer require no difficult nursing and may be cared for at home, either with or without the specialist nursing care that can be provided in the patient's home.

However, despite the fact that most of us can accept the fact that we are going to die, many people in western society spend their lives trying not to think about it and avoiding talking about it. Dying and death have become taboo subjects, not to be talked about in front of the children and especially not in front of people who are dying.

Taken together, these observations imply the possibility of a large number of people going through a period during which it is known (either by themselves or others) that they are dying and who have had little opportunity to prepare for such a period through discussion of the issues, comparison of experiences with others and so on. They also imply that a large number of people will find themselves caring for dying people with little knowledge of whether or not they are doing the right thing or how their own approach to it compares with those of other people.

These problems are often shared by professional people whose work involves them caring for the dying. Doctors and nurses, for example, have often surprisingly little training in dealing with such problems. It is only recently that books, articles and research projects on the subject of dying have become generally available. While it is to be expected that the situation for professionals will improve as expertise filters down to the earliest stages of medical, nursing and similar training, this will take time. For the general public, to take an interest in issues to do with death, dying and bereavement may be seen as excessively morbid and something to be discouraged. Yet if those who are dying and those who care for them are to function effectively, it is important that such knowledge as we have should be as widely available as possible.

Information about dying

One aspect of the taboo nature of death is that much of the information most people acquire will come through reading books and occasional magazine articles. Broadly speaking, such material can be divided into two groups. The first is the technical material written by experts for other professionals — textbooks and academic works. The other group comprises the numerous books depicting personal experiences of death. Such books are usually either personal accounts written by dying people (or those close to them), or fictional accounts of the experience of dying. With the growth in the acceptability of the subject, and the determination of particular individuals to break down the secrecy and embarrassment associated with it, each of these categories now boasts a large number of examples. Space in this chapter does not allow us, even if we were able, to discuss everything that has been written; however it is worth looking a little more closely at what books like these have to offer.

As far as technical accounts of the experience of dying are concerned, it is probably fair to remark that one person above all others has been a major influence — the psychiatrist Elisabeth Kubler-Ross. In 1969, she published a book called *On Death and Dying* which remains essential reading for professionals interested in this area, and which is also excellent for the lay reader. Although articles concerned with the experience of dying had been appearing in medical, psychological and psychoanalytic journals for decades before the appearance of her book, none had such an impact. Dr Kubler-Ross established a seminar at the University of Chicago at which various professionals — doctors, sociologists, theologians and others — considered the implications of terminal illness for the patients concerned and those caring for them. At these seminars, the patients concerned, together with relatives and hospital staff, were able to express their feelings. While it would be pointless to attempt to summarize the whole of Dr Kubler-Ross's work in a few paragraphs, it is worth considering one of her major conclusions — that the experience of the dying patient can often be described as passing through a number of stages.

On first learning that an illness is likely to be fatal, patients will commonly react by attempting to deny such news, to themselves or others. This denial may be quite open — 'The doctors say I'm dying but I don't believe it, they often make mistakes,' — or may be more subtle — 'I don't want to think about such things. I'm just going to get on with getting better.' During this stage, the person concerned may begin to experience the tremendous feeling of isolation that knowledge of dying brings. More often than not, this stage of denial and isolation will be passing, followed by a realization of the truth and an expression of anger. This anger may be rational — when the patient is not being appropriately cared for — or may be less rational, even totally irrational, as shown by patients who blame irrelevant past behaviour of their own or their relatives for their situation. Dr Kubler-Ross notes that such anger is often followed by bargaining, with hospital staff, relatives, oneself or some deity. The patient may say things like, 'I don't mind dying, but please let me keep going until my daughter's wedding.' As the illness continues, the patient may progress through depression to eventual acceptance of the situation as death comes closer.

It is important to remember, however, that these five stages will not affect everybody in the same way. Sometimes the dying person will switch between stages, alternating, say, between denial and anger. Some people may experience only a few of the stages, never for example showing any signs of denial. The majority of people are likely, throughout the whole process, to maintain some degree of hope, for a medical breakthrough, a miracle or whatever. It is important therefore to take the model as a guide, not as an unfailing indicator of what to expect when a person is dying. However, awareness of these stages can often be helpful to both the dying person and to others in making sense of what may otherwise appear to be contradictory and conflicting experiences and emotions.

Since the publication of *On Death and Dying,* a number of professionals have produced books outlining what is known about this still very uncertain topic. Scientific journals specifically concerned with the issues of death and dying have appeared, regularly reporting the results of various research projects and the like. Examples of such books and journals are listed at the end of this book. Inevitably, however, for all their professional expertise, these works remain the accounts of the observer from *outside*; the writers are those who work *with* the dying, and are not the dying people themselves.

In sharp contrast to this, a number of books have been published which give accounts of the personal experience of dying. Some of these are sensitively written works of fiction. May Sarton's book *A Reckoning*, for example, is a moving story of one woman's experience of being told that she has serious cancer with probably only a year or so to live. Other books are true accounts of dying, written either by dying people themselves or by their close loved ones. One such book of particular interest since, like this one, it is concerned with the death of a medical practitioner is *An Autumn Life*. It is an account of the death in 1982 of a surgeon, Percy Helman. Following his death, his wife discovered a number of tape recordings he had made during his illness, and, with the help of these, wrote a book describing his life up to and through this difficult time.

In *An Autumn Life*, Percy Helman and his wife describe how it felt to be told of the seriousness of the illness, his reactions to the diagnosis and treatment, his fears and anxieties, his hopes and aspirations. For many dying people, such an intense, personal account of one man's experience can provide reassurance. One of the major problems of the dying person is the loneliness their status implies; no matter how many friends the person has, the odds are they will be the only person in their group of friends with a shortened life expectancy. To be able to share experiences with another person in a similar position, if only through the pages of a book, may go some way towards relieving such loneliness.

In many respects, a book like *An Autumn Life* has advantages over the more professionally written texts like those of Dr Kubler-Ross. As a *personal* experience it may be easier for readers in a similar position to relate to what is written. The comments of an outside observer may be regarded with some scepticism. 'How could they know for sure what the dying person is thinking?' By contrast, knowing that the writer is in the same position as the reader adds an immediacy and a veracity that may be difficult for an outsider like a doctor to capture.

On the other hand, such accounts also have certain disadvantages. Perhaps most important is, again, the fact that it is a *personal* account. While this may make the book easier to relate to, it also leaves the reader with the problem of deciding how much of someone else's experience will relate to their own. In this respect, the more professional texts, dealing with observations of large numbers of individuals, may be able to give a more general overview, but at the cost of losing the intimacy and immediacy of the personal account.

It was with this problem in mind — how to capture the immediacy and honesty of a personal experience while at the same time trying to provide a book of practical value to other people in a similar position — that we decided to write the present book.

As a clinical psychologist, Glynn Owens was, like many professionals, concerned with the experience and well-being of dying people, but personally in good health, and thus always, to some extent, an outsider. As a general practitioner, Freda Naylor was also concerned in a very practical way with the experiences of dying people, but Freda was no outsider, since she knew that she too was dying of cancer. We thus found ourselves in a position to write a unique book, one which combined both professional expertise with personal experience. Our aim in writing this book has been to use a personal account of dying to indicate and illustrate practical ways of dealing with dying.

Inevitably we have had — and could have — only limited success in achieving such an aim. To be told that one's life expectancy is short is *never* going to be an easy thing to deal with. Nevertheless, we hope that people in this position and those close to and caring for them will find something to help them from what we have written. Possibly our book will go some way towards allowing people to take a more positive attitude to their illness. If so, this can only be a good thing. It has not been proven whether or not a positive attitude will actually prolong life expectancy, but the 'will to live' has been spoken of by many as a factor in survival. Its scientific study is inevitably difficult, although there does appear to be some limited scientific evidence for a link between attitude and survival. A study of breast cancer patients in London, for example, has shown lower survival rates and higher recurrences of cancer in women who became passive or hopeless following diagnosis. However, research into this is still in its preliminary stages, and much more needs to be done before definite conclusions can be drawn.

However, even if having a positive attitude doesn't improve the *quantity* of life, it is clearly likely to improve its *quality*. And, for the person who has only a relatively short time to live, this may be the most important thing of all.

Freda Naylor: a brief biography

Since much of this book is concerned with Freda's personal experiences, it may be helpful to know a little about Freda's life history. She was born in 1935 in Rawtenstall, Lancashire. She studied medicine at Manchester University, obtaining her degrees of Bachelor of Medicine and Bachelor of Surgery in 1958. The following year she married Leslie Naylor, and, in 1962, their first child, Elizabeth, was born. Their second daughter, Madeleine, was born in 1963, and their third, Phillipa, in 1964. This close and loving family was to prove a source of great help and comfort during the period of Freda's illness.

At the age of 40, after several years of doing sessional work, Freda went into general practice in Liverpool. Later she was to become closely involved in the training of other general practitioners in Liverpool, a task she approached with remarkable dedication. In 1985, she obtained financial support to enable her to spend a year at the sub-department of clinical psychology at Liverpool University's Medical School. However, just as she was about to start on what should have been an exciting and fulfilling period in her life, she was diagnosed as suffering from advanced cancer and told that she had not long to live.

Freda's response to this news was not to give up. Rather, she resolved to make use of her situation and her expertise as a doctor and teacher to help others involved in such situations. With the help of friends and colleagues she worked at passing on her experiences to others, indicating how her knowledge might help others. She gave talks, wrote articles and produced a video teaching package on communication in terminal illness. She also kept a detailed journal, much of which is reproduced in this book. While doing all this, she still continued many of her out-of-work activities and hobbies. Like her husband she was a keen photographer, and had been awarded the Licentiateship of the Royal Photographic Society in 1984. She continued with her photography during her illness, producing many beautiful pictures, and entering a number of photographic competitions. As far as her illness permitted, she maintained physical activities like walking and swimming. Her hope was that sharing her experience of dying would be of help to others. This book is part of the fulfilment of that hope.

Summary

For most of us death is not entirely unexpected and without warning. Yet, because death is a taboo subject in society, there is little opportunity for people to prepare for a period in their lives when they know themselves to be fatally ill. Nor is there any opportunity for friends and relatives to prepare for such an eventuality. Even those professionally involved in the care of the dying — doctors, nurses and others — have little preparation for how to deal with such difficult situations.

Fortunately there has been something of a trend away from treating death as a taboo subject recently. Books, magazine articles, reports of research, are all beginning to appear with greater frequency, bringing the subject of death 'out of the closet'. Technical books on death, written primarily for professionals, have done much to extend our knowledge of the subject of dying. A number of stages through which the dying person may pass in reacting to the news of a fatal illness have been identified. At the same time, accounts of the deaths of particular individuals, both fictional and non-fictional, have provided us with insight into the intensely personal experiences involved. This book is an attempt to combine the expertise of the professional with the experience of the personal. It should enable those who are dying, and those involved in their care, to learn a little about how one person dealt with the problems she encountered, and how to apply this knowledge to their own experiences.

Practical implications

The issues discussed in this chapter are *not* simply abstract and theoretical; they have practical implications for all of us. These include:

- Don't go through life pretending that you're never going to die; to do so is as unrealistic as having a morbid obsession with death. If you can acknowledge the inevitability of your own death calmly and in good time, you're likely to be able to deal with it better when, eventually, you have to face it.

- Whilst it might be comforting to think that there's no need to prepare for knowledge of dying, that one may simply die totally unexpectedly in one's sleep, this is not the most usual pattern of death. For the majority of people there will be at least a little forewarning of death, and hence a period of time when this knowledge has to be coped with.

- In a similar way, it's unrealistic to assume that caring for the dying can be left to hospitals, doctors, etc. Many people will die at home, and even those who die in hospital will usually have friends and relatives visiting them. Furthermore, it's worth remembering that few people in the medical profession receive much training in dealing with dying.

- One way to become a little better prepared is to read books and articles about death and dying. Such material may include technical works aimed largely at professionals and personal accounts, both fictional and non-fictional, aimed largely at a lay audience. A lot can be learned from these sources. Hopefully, this book will help those who, for one reason or another, find themselves dealing with dying.

2
Telling and being told

In general, we are not used to talking about death; when we do it is usually in very general terms. Rarely do we talk specifically about our own death, or that of the person to whom we are speaking. A consequence of this is that when we do have to talk about death in personal terms, most of us are ill-prepared to do so. Without practice and preparation for talking about death, our attempts to do so often turn out to be clumsy, tactless and embarrassing. Talking about death is rarely a pleasant activity, but a little careful thought can improve matters a great deal.

Breaking the news to the dying person

One of the first issues to arise regarding communication about dying concerns telling the patient. Interestingly, research tends to show that most people believe that patients who are dying should *not* be told. When professionals, doctors, health visitors and the like, are asked whether they'd tell a person who had a terminal illness, only around half report that they'd tell a businessman, less than ten percent would tell an elderly widower, and only two percent would tell a 35-year-old mother with young children. Similarly non-professionals overwhelmingly feel that it would be better not to tell the patient. Practically everyone, it seems, is disinclined to tell. The picture changes dramatically, though, when people are asked to say whether they would wish to know *themselves*. Then around 80 or 90 percent of people say that they, personally, would like to be told. It appears that most people think that they themselves would be better off for knowing, but don't realize how many other people feel the same way. While we often feel that *we* could handle the news that we are dying, we under- estimate the ability of others to cope. Given our reluctance to discuss death, of course, it's not surprising that such misunderstanding occurs. Since we don't generally talk to other people about death, it's all too easy to assume that we're the only ones who'd be able to cope.

Interestingly, a similar picture appears in studies of actual dying patients. Around 90 percent of the patients who had been told believe that it had been advantageous to know. Thus it's not only when they're healthy that people believe they'd rather know; the same applies to the majority of patients actually confronted with death. Overall the research makes it clear that, for the majority of patients, it is the right decision to tell them. Despite this, the studies show that the majority of people, professional or not, would rather the patient didn't know. A possible reason for this reluctance to tell is that it spares the feelings of the living rather than helping the dying.

It's easy to understand why people should want to believe that it's better not to tell, even when they would like to know themselves. After all, breaking bad news is never pleasant, and the news that one's life expectancy is limited is, for many people, the worst possible news. Since we usually have no idea how we'd go about breaking such news, it's very tempting to avoid the whole issue by concluding that the patient would rather not know.

Since few people, including doctors, receive much training or have much practice in breaking bad news, it's perhaps not surprising that when the need arises it's often done rather unskilfully. In Freda's case the news that she had a very serious illness came as a complete shock. Indeed, it's only as a result of her medical training that she was able to deduce from what was being said that something serious was wrong; up to this point all she had suspected was a minor back problem:

Saturday; I was crouching to get something from a low drawer when I fell over. There was a sudden spasm of pain on the right side of my back and I could hardly move. I slept that night face down on a mattress on the floor, with frequent pain killers. It was obvious by the next morning that I would have to seek medical help. Our general practitioner called in an orthopaedic surgeon who said it was probably a centrally prolapsed disc and needed traction in hospital.

I went into our District General Hospital and the pain disappeared within 24 hours, my back remaining rather stiff and weak. About the middle of the week I was in hospital, the Registrar came to me, introduced himself, and said they were going to do a bone scan.

'Is that really necessary?' I asked.

'Yes.'

'Isn't it a disc then?'

'We don't know.'

'What do you hope to find?' I asked. I really was taken aback, and as a result didn't ask the question the best way round. 'We don't know,' was his reply, and off he went.

As a doctor, Freda knew that there would have to be something seriously wrong to have a bone scan performed. Up to this point, she had expected that her pain would turn out to be the result of a minor back problem; suddenly she was presented with the realization that she might be confronted with a life-threatening disease. Clearly, the way Freda found out about her illness leaves a lot to be desired. Had it not been for her medical knowledge, she would probably not have understood the significance of doing a bone scan; presumably, the registrar realized that, as a doctor, Freda *would* see the significance, and therefore knew that she would appreciate the seriousness of the situation. Yet the brief conversation did nothing to help Freda cope with the sudden shock.

Of course, it's easy to be critical of how someone else went about an admittedly difficult task. The issue here is not to find fault with one particular individual, who was no doubt doing the best he could in the face of his own anxieties, embarrassment and lack of training for this problem. It is, however, worth learning from Freda's experience how to break such news a better way.

Perhaps the first and most important point to remember when breaking bad news is the value of adequate preparation. When faced by difficult tasks, we often find it hard to think ahead and just plunge into the problem with an attitude that we'll either sink or swim. While this may be reasonable for problems which are purely our own, this is not an appropriate attitude when we have someone else's feelings to consider. If someone's about to receive from us the news that they're dying, the least we can do is put some effort into preparing the way they're told. Such preparation may include consultation with others who know the patient, checking that all the information the patient may ask for is to hand, and arranging for a loved one to be available soon after. If you're confronted with this sort of task it does no harm to physically rehearse breaking the news, with one of your friends or colleagues playing the part of the patient. If this friend or colleague is someone who actually knows the patient, so much the better. Most people will find it difficult to 'break the news' even in this sort of artificial role-play. Whilst this difficulty increases the temptation not to bother with rehearsal, it also emphasizes how important such a rehearsal can be. After all, if it's difficult to break the news to someone who's only *pretending* to be dying, think how much more difficult it will be with the person who really *is*. Such difficulties cannot be eliminated, but a rehearsal may help to reduce them.

One major problem in breaking the news, and one which creates considerable anxiety for the person doing so, is that it's never possible to know for certain exactly how the person will react. Some patients will be shocked, others will show resignation at having their fears confirmed. Some will want to be alone, others will want a loved one with them. Some will want a great deal of information, others will be able to take in nothing more once they've been told they're dying. Of course, the better you know the patient, the more chance you have of predicting their reaction accurately. The more the person giving the bad news is trusted by the patient, the easier it is for the patient to accept or believe what is said. Bear in mind, however, what we said at the beginning of the chapter about it being all too easy to assume that while we could cope ourselves, others around us may not be so equable; often people will surprise us with their ability to take the news calmly and with dignity.

Who should be told first?

Usually the first person to know for certain that a person is dying will be the doctor in charge of the patient's treatment. Who should the doctor tell first? At the simplest level, it can be argued that it's the patient's illness, the patient's body, and that the patient not only has the right to be the first to know, but that, indeed, the patient also has the right to keep the knowledge secret from some relatives and friends. In the final analysis, it is hard to argue against the viewpoint that the information that one is dying is part of the shared, intimate knowledge between patient and doctor, and that the patient has a right to expect confidentiality to be respected in this, as in other areas of medical treatment. There are a number of arguments against this point of view. Some doctors, for example, may argue that a relative may be the person to indicate whether the patient would indeed like to know. However, as we have seen earlier, many people are mistaken in their judgement of whether their loved ones would like to be told. Since death isn't commonly talked about, it's far from certain that the relative can be expected to know what the patient's feelings are likely to be, although they may, perhaps incorrectly, feel able to guess at what the patient would prefer. Another argument in favour of consulting a relative first suggests that even if the relative isn't given the right to decide such a sensitive issue, at least she or he may be able to say something about how the patient will react. Again, however, it's important to remember that many couples may be together for forty, fifty years or more and still never talk about death; knowing how one's partner reacts to everyday situations may say nothing about reacting to news about dying. Indeed, it is far from unusual for family members to remark that they are surprised how well a dying patient is coping with the situation. Finally, it may be argued that a relative may be able to actually break the bad news better on the basis of closeness to the patient. While this is tempting, especially as it allows the responsibility for this painful task to be delegated to someone else, it will rarely be a strong argument. Firstly, the very fact of the close relationship may make it difficult for a relative to break the news, since they too will be upset. Secondly, it is common for the dying patient to want specific information about the illness, something which a relative will rarely be able to give or obtain. Finally, it should be remembered that relatives are unlikely to have any experience of performing such a task, or any training in doing so.

Overall, then, whilst there may be occasions when telling a relative before the patient may be justified, it is not a course to be embarked upon lightly; any doctor deciding to do so should first check, carefully and honestly, both their own motives for doing so and the strength of their arguments. If the patient was not dying, passing on medical information to a third party would be a serious matter and not to be done lightly. To imply that the same care and consideration need not be taken with a dying patient is to imply that the very fact of dying in itself reduces the patient's rights.

Continuing communication

An important point to remember about breaking the news is that the process of communication is a *continuing* task. Whilst it's very tempting for the doctor to finish the initial interview feeling relieved that this difficult task is over, this is not always appropriate. When patients are confronted with the news that they are dying, it is difficult for them to take in a great deal more. This does not mean, however, that once a patient's questions have ceased, there is no more to be said. As the illness continues, more and more questions will arise, and it is important that the doctor or some other professional is available to give answers to such questions. Similarly, it may be that at one time a patient will indicate that some information *should* be withheld. Under such circumstances it is important that the doctor does not assume this to be an irrevocable decision on the part of the patient. As the patient starts to come to terms with the disease, information which was unwanted at an earlier stage may now be required; the doctor must therefore be ready to provide, later, information which previously the patient didn't want to know. It was, for example, over three weeks after the original test had been performed that Freda 'plucked up the courage to ask about the bone scan — I have skull metastases [secondary growths] but not necessarily in the cerebro-spinal fluid [The fluid surrounding the brain and spinal column]'. The practitioner who plunges into telling a patient in order to 'get it over with' is likely to find that the process of communication is in fact one that may continue for weeks, months or even years.

Spreading the news to others

In general, the patient will be one of the first people to know that death is close. One of the first problems to arise is that of communicating this information to others. This involves a number of decisions. It is necessary to decide *who* needs to be told, *how* they should be told, and *when* they should be told.

There will often be people who will need to be told fairly promptly. For most people, close family members will be the first to share the news. For Freda, telling Les, her husband, enabled the two of them to discuss who else should be told, and how:

> One talking point had been who to tell and when. We felt my partner in the practice, our three children and our other closest relatives (my father and my mother-in-law, Les's brothers and sisters) should know as soon as possible, and we spent some time deciding how. Apart from our eldest daughter Elizabeth (23), all our relatives lived between one and six hours' travelling time from us.

Several points need consideration here. Firstly we see that, for Freda, it was essential that certain people were told as soon as possible. The rest of the immediate family were to be told, Freda's death being an issue which would concern all of them; similarly Freda's partner in the medical practice should know, as there was no doubt that the disease would affect Freda's working life. Secondly, we can see that Freda was concerned about the problems created by physical distance. For Freda, the physical distance involved was influential in her decision regarding who to tell, since, if at all possible, she wanted to break the news face to face, rather than in a letter or by telephone.

As things turned out, Freda was able to tell both her partner and eldest daughter face to face. Interestingly, when telling Stella, her partner in their medical practice, Freda found she needed to reassure Stella:

> *I was anxious to show Stella I appreciated the problems in having a sick partner — we had had problems of this nature before and we had discussed ways of dealing with it. I would be flexible about changes I wished to make.*

That day Freda also told Elizabeth, her daughter, who had been aware that there were some growths in the bone. Not surprisingly, the news proved upsetting:

> *We told our eldest daughter, Elizabeth. I said that the 'bobbles' in the bone — she had known they were there — were cancer. She began to cry, saying 'I might have known, with your rotten luck.' I was surprised at that, I didn't think I had rotten luck! She then asked whether she would get it — Les told her about our family history of longevity on both sides. I don't think the full implications have sunk in — we will have to go slowly.*

Not everyone could be told on such an immediate face-to-face basis however, and Freda and Les soon found themselves having to weigh the urgency of telling against the advantages of telling face to face. Freda's father, for example, was to be told face to face, but this meant a delay:

> *My dad has to be told and is being brought over by a nephew and niece, who are also close, next week. I may ring them with an outline first, but plan to tell Dad face-to-face. He has shown a lot of concern, visited me last week, written twice, sent flowers this Saturday. I don't know how he will feel — we all made assumptions that I would be around to see him out.*

By contrast, Freda felt that her daughter, Madeleine, at that time living a considerable distance away, should be telephoned fairly quickly:

> *I rang Madeleine, our 22-year-old daughter in Newcastle, tried to tell her a sort of neutral story but got upset and she cried — I said we*

had the result of the X-rays and they had found something in my
vertebrae — not what I had planned to say. Les took over, said my
vertebrae were crumbling, and if she could come home in a week or
two, it would be best.

In telephoning Madeleine, Freda discovered for herself just
how difficult communication can be.

Who and how to tell: learning from Freda's experience

From this account of Freda's experience we can see some general
points regarding the problems of who and how to tell. Perhaps the
most striking of these is the help Freda obtained from her
husband. If it is at all possible to share the news quickly with a
loved one — husband, wife or someone similarly close — this
immediately provides the dying person with support and assistance in telling others. If you are dying, once the first person has
been told, you have someone with whom you can discuss the
problems of telling others. In Freda's account of how she told
Madeleine, for example, we saw that she found the telephone
conversation difficult and became upset, but was able to hand
over to Les. The support and assistance of a loved one who shares
the problem can be a tremendous help during this difficult
period, and it is well worth talking to such a person as soon as is
reasonably possible.

This special person may also be a tremendous help in discussing who needs to be told and when. Freda's first priorities were
to tell her immediate family and her professional partner: other
people who find that they are dying may of course have different
priorities. Whatever these priorities turn out to be, one of the
most urgent tasks is to decide who needs to be told without delay.
Typically family members, even if death is not likely to be soon,
will be people who should learn about the situation at an early
stage. Particularly important here is the need to consider how
such a person would feel if they heard the news at second hand;
very likely they would be upset not only at the news itself, but also
at the thought that it had been kept from them.

We also see from Freda's accounts that, just as it is difficult for
the professional to break the news to a dying patient, so it can be
difficult for the patient to break the news to others. In talking to
Madeleine, Freda found herself skirting round the issue, not
saying what she had planned to. This is likely to be particularly

difficult when you know that the person to be told will be deeply upset by the news, especially when they have little or no reason to be prepared. Telling Elizabeth, who had known already about the 'bobbles' on the bone, wasn't quite so difficult. Many of the lessons we learned in discussing how to tell a patient in the first place are useful here. Plan ahead, allow plenty of time, accept that the listener may want to spend some time alone with the news, rehearse with a friend playing the listener, and try to have someone close at hand who can provide support — again, this may be a role for the first, special person you told.

Freda's accounts also show not only the tremendously variable way in which friends and relatives may react to the news, but also how difficult it can be to predict such reactions. Stella, Freda's partner, was able to discuss practical issues whilst Elizabeth reacted bitterly to what she saw as her mother's 'rotten luck'. The fear that the issue of death raises can be seen in Elizabeth questioning whether she, too, would have the same disease in the future.

Other family members had their own style of reaction — Pip, the youngest daughter 'went very quiet' on hearing the news; Freda's father, who hadn't thought of cancer, took the news without any sign of strong emotional reaction. This variation in reaction from others adds to the difficulty of telling, but it will probably never be possible to predict anyone's immediate reaction to the news. In telling others, then, we must be prepared to encounter a variety of responses, even from those we know well. Remember, too, that the news is a shock to others who may react in ways which seem tactless, selfish or otherwise inappropriate at the time. It is important not to read too much into such reactions, which are often more a sign of the shock than of the person's true feelings. Moreover, much of what is said may be difficult to understand. Often, for example, a terminal illness may be very slow; rarely if ever is it possible to say that a person will only live for a specific time. Even in the most severe cases, the timing of death will be uncertain, as will the course of the illness. This uncertainty may be very difficult for a listener to grasp. Commonly, the listener will want to know how long the dying person can expect to live, and to be told that it is impossible to predict this may be hard to accept.

If you find yourself in this sort of position, a useful first step is to tell a special person who can then help with spreading the news to others. The two of you can then decide between you who needs to be told without delay. Often it will be immediate family members who first spring to mind in this context; sisters and brothers, children and parents. These seem to be fairly obvious choices for telling immediately, however, it may not be so straightforward. Suppose, for example, your parents are very elderly. Do you wish to 'protect' them from the distress of knowing your plight? Whilst this may seem a kind and humane course of action, it is not one to be undertaken lightly. It is important to bear in mind several points if you are considering keeping the news from parents. Are you confident that it's really *them* you want to spare the pain, rather than sparing yourself the distress associated with telling them? Are you sure that they won't guess, or find out some other way? If they do find that you've been keeping the information from them the odds are that they'll feel very hurt and rejected. Think carefully about how you would feel in their position; whilst you'd be upset to discover that your child was dying, you'd probably want the opportunity to provide as much support and comfort as you were able. Of course there may be situations in which these issues may not arise. An elderly parent may, for example, be confused and somewhat disorientated, leading to difficulty in understanding what's being said to them. Some will themselves be dying, with a prognosis that suggests they'll be the first to die. Clearly it's not possible to give any hard and fast answer to the question of whether to tell an elderly parent; much will depend on the individual circumstances.

Corresponding problems may arise when considering whether or not young children should be told. In this case, however, the picture is complicated by recognition of the fact that the child will find out eventually. For many children, the opportunity to grieve in stages as death approaches gradually may be much easier to deal with than the sudden realization that a loved one has died with little or no warning that this was likely to happen. The child's appreciation and understanding of the concept of death is impor-tant here. Research suggests that very small children (up to about five years old) have difficulty appreciating that death is a *total* cessation of life, and that it is irrevocable. Later, up to around nine or ten years old, children may come to appreciate that death is final and irrevocable, but still have difficulty understanding that it is inevitable, feeling that death can somehow be eluded. From the age of nine or ten years upwards, most children appear to have a fairly adult concept of death, realizing both its finality and its inevitability. Of course, children will vary considerably in their understanding at any particular age, with the extent to which the parents discuss death being an important influence. Many children will have had a number of opportunities to familiarize themselves with the concept of death, with the loss of family pets, the observation of dead insects or animals. A child may indeed have as much difficulty with the concept of life as with that of death. In explaining death to a child, it may be necessary to explain what is meant by life, and to couch such an explanation in the child's own terms. To be alive is to be able to eat, to run around, to play, to talk to others; to be dead is to be unable to do any of these things. It is, of course, tempting to offer instead some euphemistic explanation, to say that death is like sleep, or that the person has gone to heaven. Typically however such 'explanations' are unsatisfactory for the child. If death is a hard concept to grasp, how much harder is a concept of heaven, about which even the adults cannot agree? The child who is told that the dead person is 'sleeping' may simply be placed in a situation of assuming that the dead person will, eventually, awaken. Conversely, there may be a risk with some young children that equating death with sleep will lead them to think that sleeping carries the risk of dying, leading them to fear going to sleep.

It is important to understand that, without some appreciation of the loss involved in death, of its finality, it may be very difficult for the child to grieve. Yet many therapists believe that if a child is unable to grieve successfully in such a situation, the unexpressed grief will lead to problems later in adult life. Certainly a child who is told honestly about the impending death of a loved one will need some emotional support, like anyone else in such a situation; but the child who is 'protected' from these issues is, as often as not, likely to feel excluded from what is going on, to be just as hurt by the eventual loss, but to feel that hurt even more because of the additional feelings of exclusion and isolation. It is worth remembering here, incidentally, that euphemistic accounts of death may be irritating to the dying person — as Freda commented:

> *At one point, I suddenly thought that I don't want people making inane comments about having gone to heaven — I haven't gone anywhere, I've died. I got very angry at this sugary avoidance of death. I realize, however, that I don't necessarily have the right to specify what parents say to their children.*

Describing the dying person's experience in terms of 'sleeping' or 'going to heaven' may make them quite angry, as they see their daunting and frightening experience being dismissed and trivialized, a denial of the enormity of their task.

Besides the immediate family there may be others who need to be informed quickly. Special friends or 'key' colleagues may need to be told. For example, as we have seen, Freda was keen to let Stella, her partner in the practice, know as soon as possible.

At one time, it might also be appropriate to think of people who definitely should *not* be told. Such a remark by seem incongruous, given what we have said about the possible advantages of telling and the disadvantages of not telling. Yet, on consideration, you may find that there are certain individuals whom you feel you should not tell. Your reasons may vary from simply feeling that it is none of that person's business to feeling that it may be disruptive or harmful to the relationship that already exists. Freda, for example, made an early decision not to tell the patients in the practice, feeling that this could interfere with the doctor-patient relationship. The patients, she felt, had enough to deal with in their own difficulties, without having to take account of hers as well. Moreover, the possibility existed that patients might have felt inhibited about talking about some issues (e.g. their own fear of death). For some people it may not be clear whether or not telling would be a good idea; remember that it's always possible to change your mind about *not* telling, whereas you can't change your mind once you've told someone. Again, if you're unsure about telling someone, it may be appropriate to discuss this with someone close to you or to them.

How to tell

Once it has been decided *who* needs to be told right away, the question arises of *how* these people should be told. The most obvious options are to tell people directly, face to face; to telephone the news; to write a letter; or to ask someone else (your special ally?) to do any or all of these for you.

As mentioned earlier, if you are going to break the news to others, it's a great help to plan exactly how and when you're going to do so. It may be tempting, when you meet someone, to wait until an opportunity arises before raising the issue — to wait until the 'time is right'. Remember, though, that there's *never* a right time for news like this, especially if the person you want to tell has no reason to suspect what's happened. In Freda's words, 'If you can't find an opportunity, you *make* one.'

In general, telling people face to face is probably to be preferred. Unless both people have a remarkably good telephone style it's likely that the telephone call won't go entirely as planned — as illustrated by Freda's difficulty talking to Madeleine. Further illustration of the difficulties of telephone conversation can be seen in the first indications to Freda that she definitely had cancer:

I was first told by telephone by the orthopaedic consultant that I would have to see an 'oncologist', that is to say 'I have cancer'. I felt a shock, the word 'oncologist' jarred. I felt myself to be without control over the state of my health.

It might appear that the difficulties of keeping the telephone conversation under control could be solved by writing a letter instead, writing, rewriting and checking until it looks right. Letters, however, are also less than perfect. It takes at least a day or so for a letter to reach its destination — although, for many people, this won't be too serious a problem, as often the urgency won't be such as to make a single day critical. A much more serious problem, however, is that the recipient of a letter can't ask questions. When speaking in person, or on the telephone, the questions that spring to the listener's mind can be dealt with immediately; communication by letter is inevitably slow, and, in practice, most of the people receiving such a letter are likely in any case to telephone if possible. Lastly, of course, it's important to remember that to receive such a letter may be quite a shock, and that it's impossible to predict exactly how the recipient will react. In talking face to face, or on the telephone, the possibility exists, in theory, of helping the person being told to get over the initial shock.

The last possibility, that of persuading someone else to spread the news, may be tempting since it might seem less awkward when the person most concerned isn't actually present. But, even without the quite natural dislike many people have of being talked about when they're not there, there remain problems. Although the awkwardness during the initial discussion may be reduced a little because of the absence of the patient, this awkwardness will still be there when the face-to-face meeting eventually occurs. Indeed, this awkwardness will probably be increased, since the very fact that the news was passed on through a third person will suggest that the patient is finding it difficult to cope; if, by face-to-face discussing, close relative and friends can be reassured that the dying person *is* handling the situation, the odds are that future meetings will become progressively easier.

In general, then, the best way will usually be for the dying person to pass on the news, face to face, to those who are close as soon as possible. When urgency and distance rule out telling face to face, the telephone or a letter should be seriously considered, ideally with a face-to-face meeting as soon as possible afterwards. The presence, support and assistance of someone who already knows can be a great help.

Once the news has been passed on to those with an urgent need to know, there will remain others who should know in no immediate hurry. Such people may include friends who are only seen occasionally, acquaintances, friends of friends and so on. Here it may be appropriate, and indeed necessary, to communicate by letter. This was the strategy adopted by Freda, for example, in telling friends with whom she had only occasional contact by letter, the sort of friends who would normally be sent a letter every Christmas passing on news. The knowledge that she was dying prompted Freda and Les to prepare carefully a special letter to be sent to their friends breaking the news:

> *Before and during our Canadian holiday she had some back trouble, and on the Saturday before the course started, she fell and had to go into hospital for a week for traction for what was thought to be a slipped disc. However, the tests showed she had a collapsed vertebra due to cancer secondaries. This news, of course, has been a great blow to us as there is little chance of recovery.*
>
> *We were in a unique position, however, to be able to face the facts as we know them, and have shared the news with our relatives, friends and colleagues, believing they would wish to support us. It has been a wonderful experience to receive so much help and has enabled us to come to terms with the future and to overcome problems as they have arisen.*
>
> *I have now had a course of radiotherapy to the spine and am receiving a course of cytotoxic drugs by injection. I am better at present than since I fell, so it appears that I am responding to treatment. The problems of pain and stiffness meant that I was slow to integrate myself into the course that was planned, but the decision to continue in a modified form seems to have been the right one. I had already arranged for a locum to take my place in the practice for a year, and all is running smoothly there. For my special project on the course, I hope to make a video tape for teaching purposes on communication in terminal care.*
>
> *Elizabeth, Madeleine and Phillipa have been most supportive and have made big efforts to spend time with us despite all their activities.*

[Excerpt from the first 'Naylor Newsletter', sent out at Christmas to various friends and relatives].

Of course, not everyone will want to send out a duplicated letter. Nevertheless, we can see from Les and Freda's version how such correspondence can be phrased. Carefully worded, a letter passing on the news can be greatly appreciated; recipients of the above letter described themselves as 'privileged to be included in your circle of family and friends', and 'filled with admiration for the courage and faith which shone through the letter'.

Thus if you *are* presented with the news that you are going to die in the foreseeable future, there are a number of ways in which you might make it easier to go about spreading this news to others. An ally is extremely useful, and if there is someone close to you with whom you can discuss these issues, this is likely to be a great help. The two of you should then discuss who is to be told, when they are to be told, and how they are to be told.

The question of who to tell and who not to tell will often need to be addressed fairly quickly. In considering this issue, guard against the tendency to avoid telling people unless you're sure that it really is in your and their best interests not to know; a useful strategy here is to try to imagine how they will feel when they eventually find out (as they undoubtedly will). Consider the advantages and disadvantages of telling face to face, by telephone, by letter or through a third person, and select for each of the people who has to know the method best suited to them and their circumstances. Be prepared for a variety of reactions; the shock of the news will affect people differently.

How might others react?

As we saw earlier in the chapter, professionals often feel awkward telling people that they are fatally ill, in part because it's not obvious how they will react. The same problem arises when the dying person has to pass the news on to others. How might they react when they are told the news? We've seen from Freda's accounts earlier in the chapter how the immediate reactions of other people can vary tremendously. The emotional control shown by Freda's father, Elizabeth's tears, Stella's discussions all illustrate the different ways in which people may show their initial reaction. For some, the news may be a total shock if they have no inkling of the possibility of fatal illness. Others may have suspected the possibility, but will nevertheless feel shocked when their suspicions are confirmed.

Because receiving such news can be such a shock, it is difficult to predict how anyone will react even if we think we know them well. It is, however, important to note that the person's immediate reaction may reflect the shock itself more than anything else. It is therefore important not to infer too much from immediate reactions. Often someone may appear to be uncaring, unsympathetic or unmoved on first being told the news. A response may appear on the surface to reflect primarily self-concern. It is important that these reactions are seen in the context of the person dealing with a shock, and not as indicative of their true feelings in any straightforward way. Nor should it be seen as predicting how that person will continue to respond once the initial shock has worn off.

Having said all this, it remains the case that, by and large, most people who are told will want to be helpful and supportive. An apparently tactless or inconsiderate reaction will often reflect nothing more than the person's confusion about the sort of reaction which is appropriate. Just as we rarely discuss how to react to news of our own approaching death, we have little opportunity to learn how to react when told of someone else's. Partly this reflects the tremendous variety of human needs and experience, making it difficult to lay down strict and specific guidelines on how to take such news. Having said this, however, a few general points are worth considering:

- *Do* let the person break the news in their own time.
- *Do* remember that listening can be as important as speaking.
- *Do* admit it if you feel awkward or embarrassed; attempts to cover this up are more likely to be misinterpreted.
- *Do* allow the person to talk about it.
- *Do* ask any factual questions you think are important — for example, about treatment, prognosis, etc.
- *Do* feel able to ask how they are taking the news themselves.

- *Don't* try to steer the conversation away from death; this doesn't necessarily provide comfort, but merely gives the impression that discussion isn't allowed.
- *Don't* feel awkward if the person shows signs of being upset or begins to cry; rather make it clear that they're allowed to do so if they wish.
- *Don't* make offers of help unless you're sure you'll be able to fulfil them; if you are sure, ask what, if anything, you can do to help.
- *Don't* pass on the news to others unless this has been specifically agreed.
- *Don't* demand a justification of the person's earlier behaviour

— for example, 'Why didn't you tell me before?'

● *Don't* start to treat the person as helpless, needing everything doing for them.

Just as the reactions of the dying person will change and adapt, so will those of the people sharing this knowledge. The immediate need, particularly if the patient has only recently been given the news, is for everyone to work together in dealing with it. Remember that for many people, a major concern about dying is for those who will be left behind; often the dying person will be as keen to help others deal with the news as the others are to help them — as we saw in Freda's reassurance of Stella, her partner in the practice. Under such circumstances all can work together to provide mutual support.

Summary

Communication in terminal illness is a complex business. In the first instance, there is the problem of telling the patient that they are dying. This is usually done by a professional who ought to regard it as an ongoing task rather than as a 'one-off' encounter. The patient then has to tell other people; usually it is helpful if the first person to be told can be someone particularly close, who can then act as an ally in discussing the problems of telling others. Some people will need to be told as soon as possible, others with less urgency. It will not always be possible to tell everybody face to face — some people will have to be told by telephone, letter or through a third person. The particular method of communication chosen will depend on the specific circumstances. Finally, there is the issue of how friends and family might react to the news that someone close to them has a limited life expectancy. Such news will come as a shock to many, and will confront most people with a situation with which they are unfamiliar and in which they are unsure how to react. Immediate reactions should, therefore, be interpreted with caution, and not necessarily seen as a reflection of their true feelings.

Practical implications

Many of the issues discussed above have practical implications for communication about dying. Such communication will never by easy. However, the difficulties can be reduced if we take account of the following:

- Pretending that the dying patient would rather not know is rarely helpful. Evidence suggests that most patients would prefer to know if they are dying, and it should not be assumed otherwise without good reason. Telling people they are dying may be difficult, but keeping the news from them is even more so.

- When breaking such news, prepare and plan carefully, and allow adequate time. If possible, rehearse with a friend or colleague playing the patient. Be prepared for the communication to be a continuing task over the remainder of the person's life.

- If you are given the news that your own life may be limited, be prepared to take in information one step at a time. Feel free to ask for further information as and when you require it, even if previously you've said you'd rather not know.

- Try to tell someone especially close to you as soon as possible; if you'd like help in doing so, feel free to ask the person who told you. Discuss with this especially close person who else should know, and how and when they are to be told. Be determined in passing on the news; don't be tempted to wait for the right time — there isn't one.

- Beware the temptation *not* to tell people — whilst this will sometimes be appropriate, remember that they will find out anyway. On the other hand, remember that deciding not to tell someone doesn't mean you can't change your mind later.

- Be prepared for a variety of reactions from others, but beware of reading too much into them.

- If you receive the news that a loved one is dying, be as honest and as open as you can, both about your own feelings and those of others. Acknowledge that it's going to be a difficult time for everyone, and try to help each other to cope.

3
Dealing with dying: Early responses

In chapter 1 we noted that people may respond in a variety of ways to the news that they are dying. The stages noted by Elisabeth Kubler-Ross: denial, anger, bargaining, depression and acceptance, describe common aspects of the individual's response. It is important to remember that, for many people, the process of dying will be a long one, the length of time between being informed that one is dying and one's actual death being uncertain and unpredictable. For many people, there will be a difference between people's early reactions and their later responses once there has been a chance to become more accustomed to the news. In the same way, the responses of others to being told that someone close to them is dying will vary with time. In considering responses to such news, it is useful to consider early responses and later responses separately.

Being told: early reactions

In Freda's account of being told that she had cancer and that it was untreatable, we can see some of the elements of a typical immediate reaction. In particular, we see Freda trying hard to deny the evidence in front of her. Her medical training told her that the intention to do a bone scan implied that something was seriously wrong; yet when she later saw the consultant and discussed the X-ray photographs which indicated the need for a bone scan, she tried hard to avoid a pessimistic interpretation:

> *The consultant came about 5:30 bringing the X-rays. He showed me some lytic lesions [areas where the tissue of the bone was breaking down] on the pubic ramus. I looked at the spine and said, 'And the disc is narrow, isn't it?'*

'Yes.'

'Are we looking at two different things?'

'No.'

I had not seen what was an osteolytic lesion in the vertebra, although there was enough information to make the connection. I didn't want to, so suppressed it.

What we see in this account is Freda attempting to deny the evidence of her senses and her knowledge. 'I didn't want to, so suppressed it.' It is perhaps inevitable that information such as this, with its obvious impact on a person's self-concept and view of the future cannot be taken in straightforwardly and simply. Information of this nature needs to be taken in in steps; not everything can be taken in at once.

It is interesting to note here that looking back, Freda was able to remember a similar experience of denial much earlier. Several months before her diagnosis, Freda had noticed a lump in her left breast, worried that this might be cancer and consulted her GP and a specialist.

I was interested in my reactions at that time. After I first felt it [the lump] and thought 'perhaps malignant', I deliberately didn't think about it for a few hours, then rang my GP.

Again we can see here how it is tempting to avoid thinking about the problem, taking it in only bit by bit.

As time goes on, however, most people will find themselves moving from a stage of denying the fatal illness altogether, through regarding this as a possibility, to increasing degrees of acceptance. Talking to others may influence this process either way; if the listener simply agrees with the patient when they deny their illness acceptance may be delayed. On the other hand, if the listener is open to discussion of the fears and anxieties, this may help the person to come to terms with the news:

The bone scan was booked for the following Tuesday and by then, on discussing it with my husband and thinking about it, I was very concerned. I was fairly sure then that I had bony secondaries, that the cancer had spread and was attacking the bones.

Even then it is important to note that acceptance may still not be total. Remember that when Freda was told by telephone that an appointment had been made with an oncologist (a cancer specialist) the word itself still jarred.

At this time the person may remain in much the same psychological state for some time, or may change relatively quickly. For Freda, her medical knowledge gave her a lot to think about regarding the actual course of the disease, thinking which led her fairly soon to a stark acceptance of reality:

> *Obviously I had fears about damage to the spinal cord and thought about it in the night. One night I woke up thinking 'You are going to die.'*

Another way in which night-time may provide the setting for the beginning of acceptance is in the person's dreams:

> *I dreamt I was in some sort of unstable vehicle, didn't recognize it . . . then I found it was a plane and I was due to parachute out, without a parachute.*

It doesn't take a great deal of perception to identify the symbolism of such a dream. The unstable, unrecognizable vehicle can be seen as reflecting Freda's body, parachuting out suggesting leaving of this body — her approaching death. The fact that she is leaving the plane without a parachute clearly reflects the loneliness of dying, the fact that this is something which must be done without the love and support of others who have helped us through so many other difficulties. Freda's description of the plane as unstable and unrecognizable mirrors her more conscious thoughts about her body at this time:

> *I have been doing a lot of thinking, less weeping as time goes on. Some worrying about what was happening to my body — I could no longer trust it.*

As, gradually, the realization of the fatal illness was assimilated, Freda found her thoughts becoming more and more directly concerned with the disease and her prognosis:

> *During all these 'workings through' I thought if I could keep saying 'I am still me' it would help.*

The notion that one can no longer trust one's own body is, of course, a difficult one to accept, since it immediately raises the problem of one's own identity. Freda, recognizing that 'her body' and 'herself' were no longer synonymous, found it helpful to remind herself that, despite what was happening to her body, she was still the same person.

Of course, it is inevitable that, once a person starts to accept that they have a fatal illness, they will start to pay attention to practical, as well as emotional, issues. Most obvious are thoughts about how advanced the disease might actually be, and how it will progress:

> *Should I be worrying now about cerebral secondaries [spread of the cancer to the brain] and about fitness to drive? Will changes come gradually or quickly?*

And:

> *How long will I be able to read or write — does that leave me as just a chatterbox?*

Again, Freda soon found the benefits of having been open with Les, her husband, about her illness, since they were able to discuss practical issues effectively:

> *I talked this evening about changes for Les after my death. Our house will be big and expensive but decided that an early move would not be a good thing on principle. He doesn't feel he wants 'lots of strangers' around as tenants. We moved on to the question of Les wishing to remarry. He has already thought about this and thinks he will not find anybody. I wanted to make it clear that he can if he wishes — it's a waste if he doesn't!*

Although this isn't to say that such a conversation isn't to some extent distressing:

> *I had one fleeting glance . . . of the family going on living without me — I felt quite excluded.*

Indeed, it's important to remember that, although Freda is clear about being 'still me', this isn't to say that life can now go back to what it was before the diagnosis. While it might be tempting to aim simply to 'carry on as before', this will rarely be practical. Freda, for example, while remaining essentially the same person, noted a number of significant changes. We have already seen how she felt she could no longer trust her body. As a result of this, she found herself becoming very upset if things went wrong, as she remarked one day after a mix-up about the day of her radiotherapy treatment:

> *It's funny how silly things upset and annoy. I feel very vulnerable.*

The realization that one is dying produces so many changes that, for most people, it will be impossible to ignore the facts of one's illness and carry on as before. There may well be physical constraints which prevent this — Freda for example found that her stiffness affected her neck, making aspects of driving difficult, and later caused difficulty in walking. Treatment, too, can produce its own physical difficulties. For example, certain anticancer drugs may, for a while, produce hair loss, making the wearing of a wig a new part of life.

Even without these physical constraints, however, the psychological impact of the news that one is dying is imposible to ignore. Freda found many worries and concerns needed to be overcome. These included anxiety, panic and fear — fear of pain, fear of loss of dignity, fear of loneliness. Such negative emotions may be exacerbated by the large element of uncertainty present in such situations. And most profoundly, as Freda put it:

> *One is changed by the knowledge of one's future — one asks, 'What do I want to do in the time I have left?'*

A considerable amount of time will inevitably be spent trying to make sense of the fact that one is dying, looking back to come to a better understanding and to try to find causes. Freda found herself wondering about whether the stresses to which she'd earlier been exposed — preparation for a period of study leave, a holiday in Canada — might have played a part in her illness:

> *The admission nurse and Senior House Officer were both very pleasant. The SHO asked me about recent stress — she had found it a factor when working on oncology in India. I think preparation for the study leave and the Canadian trip were stressful . . . I think I might have lived longer if we had not gone — too late now!*

Similarly it is not surprising that close attention is paid to any changes in the way one feels, as a clue to how the disease is progressing. Freda found herself reflecting on the extent to which one feels, subjectively, that there has been a change in the disease before it is detected by tests. On having fluid drawn from her spinal column to check for spread of the cancer, for example, she noted:

> *The lumbar puncture was painless and the cerebro spinal fluid [the fluid from the spine] was clear. I reckon it has to be quite far gone to be cloudy — the first indications always being subjective. However, I don't wish to spend time wishing myself into more complications; I am now beginning treatment with some hope.*

At times, Freda found her thought processes surprising even herself. On thinking of the tumour as part of her body but somehow separate, she noted during a period of ravenous appetite:

Living while dying

I thought of a bizarre joke I can only write — I am eating for more than one.

Learning from Freda's experience

What can we learn from Freda's experience of her early responses to diagnosis? Perhaps the most obvious point to note is that there is a period following learning the news which is characterized by a considerable amount of adjustment. The first part of this adjustment is likely to be concerned with the assimilation of the facts of the situation at a rate the person can handle. To take in everything at once is too much to expect, so the person is likely to indulge in some degree of denial in the beginning. For Freda this was illustrated by, for example, refusing to see certain aspects of the X-rays with which she was presented, despite the fact that she was adequately qualified to make such judgements. Even when information is taken in, there may still be dissociation between the intellectual recognition of a fact and acknowledging it emotionally — what Freda has described elsewhere as, 'knowing but not acknowledging'.

It is important to recognize that this gradual assimilation of the situation, from denial to acceptance, is a quite natural and normal process. If you are given such news, you are likely to be rather stunned, even if you have already had your suspicions. If, like Freda, the news comes completely out of the blue, you will obviously find it difficult to take anything in. You should consider it appropriate that it will take some time to get used to the whole idea and that, for a while at least, you may wish to avoid the whole issue, or try to put the most optimistic interpretation imaginable on what is happening.

In time, however, and particularly if you are able to discuss the matter with someone who is close to you, it is likely that subconsciously, at least, the reality of death will be acknowledged. As Freda found though, this brings its own mental turmoil. Inevitably the issue of death is likely to become a dominant theme in one's thoughts. Dreams may be disturbing as the half-conscious awareness of one's vulnerability struggles to break through into consciousness. There is likely to be considerable uncertainty, and a general feeling of insecurity. Here, the support of others may be particularly helpful. A colleague discussing Freda's problems with her remarked that at the time she seemed to be 'relying on external resources'. While agreeing with this analysis, Freda however noted that, 'As I feel very empty, this seems a reasonable reaction!' Indeed, if the resources are there, and the support is being offered, it makes sense to draw on them. The whole process is likely to be difficult and there is no point in refusing help and thereby increasing the difficulties one is facing.

Once the person starts to acknowledge the reality and imminence of death, many questions are likely to arise. Most important to a lot of people in this situation is *exactly* how much longer they will live. This question is of tremendous importance, but it is likely that any honest answer a doctor gives will be unsatisfactory to the patient. With terminal illnesses in general there is tremendous uncertainty about the future course of the illness. This is especially true of cancer. For example, a month or so after Freda's diagnosis, one doctor guessed that her life expectancy might be a few months at the worst, perhaps a year at the best, yet over eighteen months later Freda was still alive and working on this book! The reality is that *any* estimate of how long a person has to live is little more than an educated guess, and considerable uncertainty is unavoidable. Yet during the course of her illness Freda has found that 'uncertainty can be faced, can be lived with. The passage of time uneventfully confirms and reassures.'

Once the notion of death begins to be accepted, some degree of preoccupation with the future course of the illness becomes almost inevitable. Many questions are likely to occur to the dying person, some of which may be too frightening to discuss. How much pain will be involved? What will be the first signs that things are taking a turn for the worse? What treatments are available, and what are their side-effects? Will the disease affect mobility, thought processes, the ability to walk and talk? Many such questions may occur to the dying person. Often the thought of what the answer might be will make the question too frightening to ask. Again it's important here to remember that, as time goes by, many things may change, and, that as the idea begins to be accepted, so some of the questions which were too frightening to ask will now require answers.

Besides questions regarding the future course of the illness, it's also possible at this stage that the person may struggle to make sense of what has happened. In particular, there may be an effort to pinpoint a cause of the disease, to look back over one's life in an effort to see where one went 'wrong'. To look for this sort of meaning is perfectly natural. Our society leads us to develop a sort of implicit theory about the justice of the world we live in. Often we like to believe that if something bad happens to someone, then they must have done something to deserve it. Thus, when something bad happens to *us*, we start to ask what we have done to deserve it. This was apparent in Freda's thoughts about whether stress might have brought on the illness: did the stress of preparing for her study leave, or of taking a major trip abroad precipitate the disease? Of course, the reality is that practically all serious illnesses are the result of a large number of causes. They may be physical, emotional, environmental, or genetic, all of which may interact in a highly complex way. Nevertheless, the notion that there is one specific thing which is *the* cause of one's illness is likely to occur to many people in this situation. It is important to remember that this is a perfectly normal response, an attempt on the part of the person to rationalize what is happening to them. Sometimes such thoughts may leave the person feeling guilty about what has happened. Here again, the opportunity to talk it over with another person may be a considerable help.

Basically, the initial stages of responding to the news that one is dying can be seen as a process of adaptation to a new situation. One of the most striking aspects of this new situation is the high degree of uncertainty involved. For most of us, through most of our lives, there is relatively little uncertainty. There is always the *outside* possibility of things not going as we expect, but the degree of uncertainty is usually miniscule in comparison with the uncertain world of the dying person. The very uncertainty of whether or not one will still be alive in a week, a month, a year is something which the rest of us do not worry about. In addition, however, it is important to remember that, even with considerable help and support, dying is inevitably a lonely business. This loneliness, this isolation means that there is a limit to which others can relieve the dying person of uncertainties — for after all, they're not in a position to know. This feeling of uncertainty, and the adaptation to it, may cause considerable anxiety to the dying person at this time. The problem may be made worse as even one's own thoughts start to be surprising and to seem sometimes out of control — as with Freda's joke about eating for two. Yet, as Freda discovered, with time and the support of others, it is possible to learn to cope with the uncertainty.

One of the major tasks during this period of adaption is dealing with the anxieties which arise regarding those who will be left behind. Perhaps surprisingly, the notion that death is worse for those who remain than for those who die is accepted by many people in our society. (It's one of those things which we often think only *we* believe: because we don't talk about death, we never have the chance to find out how many people agree with us.) This problem is one which may be made considerably easier by having a close loved one with whom issues can be discussed. For Freda, the opportunity to discuss matters with her husband not only enabled her to share many of her own fears and anxieties about dying, but also to relieve herself of many of the concerns she had for him and for the rest of her family.

By now it should be clear that, tempting as it may be to think that one can carry on as if nothing had happened, there really is quite a lot to do at this stage. The patient has to go through the process of assimilating the knowledge, both consciously and unconsciously, in a series of steps. It will be difficult, if not impossible, to give anything more than a very vague answer to the question, 'How long have I got?' This vagueness highlights the tremendous uncertainty with which the dying person has to cope. Similar uncertainties will arise regarding the course of the disease. The fact that there may be major changes in patterns of dreams adds further to the uncertainties and anxieties of this period, as does the way in which even one's own thoughts may be surprising. The news that one is dying is inevitably going to dominate the person's thinking for a while. There may be feelings of guilt, or thoughts of, 'where did I go wrong?' And, of course, there are likely to be many anxieties about the loved ones to be left behind.

Clearly, then, this is a time for rethinking priorities. Time is more limited than one thought, and it's appropriate to think carefully about what is to be done in the remaining time available — what 'unfinished business' needs to be completed. Here again we see the value of having a close ally, a loved one with whom things can be discussed. Such a person can do much to help with setting priorities, talking over the possibilities and helping the options to become clearer.

One's close ally can be a tremendous help in other ways as well. This is a time when uncertainty is a major problem. Anything which can help to reduce this uncertainty may have tremendous value. Some uncertainties are inevitable, since no-one can answer questions such as, 'What is it like to die?' Some issues will continue to be largely uncertain for most of the period of dying, even how much longer the patient can expect to live, but many uncertainties can be considerably reduced or eliminated by discussion with one's ally. Uncertainties about how those left behind will cope, for example, may be greatly relieved by discussing them. Even the uncertainties about such things as random thoughts are likely to be reduced if issues have already been brought out into the open. Often random thoughts can surprise us, and make us uncertain about even our own thinking, but they also reflect issues which we're not trying to face up to — as we see in the disturbance of dreams. By discussing them and bringing them out into the open, random thoughts and dreams can be substantially reduced if not totally dispelled. Finally, at a time when the setting of priorities becomes more important than ever before, the knowledge that one has discussed these priorities with someone close makes one much less likely to be anxious or uncertain about them.

For the dying person, then, a close ally is of tremendous value in getting through this period of adaptation. The need for such a person highlights the fact that this is also a period of adaptation for the friends, relatives and associates of the dying person. In looking at this period, then, it is useful also have have a brief look at the way in which family and friends may react.

The reactions of others

Despite the fact that everyone, eventually, dies, most people have little experience of dealing with people who are in the process of dying as opposed to death. A family member may have died suddenly, from a heart attack or accident, or a friend may have had a fatal illness whilst being deceived by doctors and family into believing that it is not serious. In consequence, people commonly have little idea how to behave when confronted with a *dying* person. The result is that, like their immediate reactions, the short-term adaptation of others may vary considerably. For example Les, Freda's husband, very soon started to take practical steps:

> *Les was obviously working on practical lines. Within a fortnight of my first back pain he had changed our beautifully soft double bed for the firmer twin beds he had made a few months previously for the guest room, so we were now sleeping side by side again! He is also thinking through possible alterations to the house, and getting me a disabled parking sticker.*

Others seemed reluctant to accept the reality of the situation, perhaps thinking that they should set an example to the dying person. Freda however found herself acutely sensitive to the difference between maintaining a realistic hope or at least not giving up without a fight, and the 'clutching at straws' fantasy of a miracle cure:

I felt I had to put M. right that there was no possibility of cure . . . the word 'miracle' was mentioned . . . okay, but it's a small chance and at present it seems cruel to hope!

Dealing with a person who is dying raises a number of distressing feelings in many healthy people. Such feelings may include depression and anxiety (being reminded of their own mortality), guilt and inadequacy. A common way of attempting to deal with such feelings is to distance oneself from the dying person by putting them into a helpless, almost child-like role. Not only does this enable the dying person to be seen as very different (and hence less likely to remind oneself of one's own mortality) but also appears to provide many opportunities to 'do things' for them. Unfortunately this is not as successful as one might hope:

One of my friends insisted, despite my protest, in accompanying me across the car park and tried to offer to hold what I was carrying — two small objects! I became very irritable as I feel quite pressurized by 'let me help' and 'how are you?' — I had to speak quite directly, probably hurtfully.

Other friends, unable to cope with the situation, may begin to distance themselves from the dying person, and may even totally avoid any further meetings.

A major reason for such unsatisfactory encounters is that in general, as we mentioned earlier, most people simply do not know how to react. Recognizing this, Freda met the problem head on, as she describes in this account of a visit by a friend:

Lovely to see her, even if she did have to make her own coffee and do her washing up. She told me I am making it easier for people to help me by being direct.

Similarly when one of her daughters changed her mind about going away for a weekend:

I told her I was pleased, but that she must never stay with me just for duty if she felt it was difficult. She said with great conviction that she wanted to stay. I told her how I was enjoying her company — very relaxing — and to think we used to fight!

It is all too easy to forget how much a fatal illness separates one from other people, making it necessary to be explicit about things which one might have hoped to take for granted. The result is that often things need to be said out loud, as Freda noted from discussion with her eldest daughter:

She is very clear that she wishes to treat me just the same ... I
suppose it's a measure of the separateness that illness brings that it
has to be said — it seemed to be helping to say I am just the same
(mainly) so that people feel at ease with it.

The early responses of others: Learning from Freda's experience

Clearly the process of adaptation has its problems for others as
well as for the dying person. For friends and relatives it will seem
that, all of a sudden, a gulf has opened up between themselves
and the person with the illness. For the dying person, this gulf is a
daunting prospect, emphasizing the loneliness of their situation.
A great temptation is to take the illness as meaning that the person
is no longer to be left in control of their remaining life. Everything
is to be done for them, every decision made. For the dying person,
however, this may be the opposite of what is really required. The
struggle to maintain an identity, a sense of self, makes it essential
that people respond appropriately. Certain things may no longer
be possible, or may be things which the person would clearly not
wish to do; help with these is likely to be welcomed. But, at all
times, it is important to allow the dying person to live life to the
full. This includes being allowed to continue doing those things
which they can and not thrusting them instantly in a position of
helplessness. Avoiding the issue doesn't help, nor does assuming
that the person has suddenly become totally incapable. Unless
there are *very* good reasons for doing otherwise, the dying person
should continue to be treated with the dignity, rights and respon-
sibilities of any other adult. The need is less for sympathy than
empathy, an attempt to understand how the dying person is
feeling and a willingness to help by sharing the experience. Such a
reaction was highlighted for Freda by the reaction of her psychologist colleagues:

> *I am interested in the way the psychologists received my news — very*
> *openly, no 'sympathy' — empathy, yes, makes it easier, very matter*
> *of fact.*

For the dying person, the difficulties experienced by others at
this time only add to the existing problems of coping with the need
to adapt during this period. As with the immediate reactions of
others, it is probably unwise to read too much into their short-
term response. Confusion and uncertainty about the right thing
to say or do will often result in awkwardness. Often friends will be

reluctant to discuss the issue of dying, feeling that this may somehow remind the person that this is happening. In such circumstances, it may be necessary to point out, as gently as possible, that dying people cannot just forget the fact that they are dying; rather, it will always be hovering on the periphery of one's thoughts. To hope that if a friend doesn't talk about death it will be forgotten for a while is unrealistic and unfair; most dying people prefer that their friends speak naturally and easily, not constantly guarding against any reference to death or dying.

In a similar way, friends may be reluctant to discuss practical matters, despite the fact that these may be of overwhelming importance to the dying person. Often there is a feeling that to be concerned with such things is somehow callous or heartless. Yet, as with the issue of dying, such matters cannot be left to look after themselves. The dying person will, perhaps soon, have to confront them anyway, and will usually do so more easily having shared the problem with others.

What this means is that it may often be wise for the dying person to put some effort into explaining, very clearly, how friends and relatives should behave. If you are dying, and the prospect of friends struggling to avoid the subject in any conversation is not a pleasant one, it may be a good investment at this stage to spell out for them that to talk about death is, if not actually welcome, at least very acceptable. In such a situation death is unlikely to be far from your thoughts. Explain this to your friends, and tell them that you'd like to share your thoughts with them. If practical problems are worrying you, it may be helpful to tell friends and relatives about them; if (as Les did with Freda) they anticipate practical problems for you, thank them for their help in solving them. Remember that terminal illness creates an inevitable barrier between the sick and the healthy and that it is to be expected that people will be unsure how to react to you. Remember that even those who say and do the right things may not be as confident as they seem, and may be glad of reassurance. Others, whose behaviour is not as you would wish, can be guided gently or told straight out how you would like them to behave. If, for example, a friend appears to be embarrassed when the issue of death arises, bring the issue out into the open. Say something like, 'You know, I get the feeling that you're uncomfortable about the topic of death, that you're avoiding it. Perhaps it's worth saying that I'd much rather it was something we could talk about, even if at times it might be upsetting. I may sometimes cry if we discuss it. Although I may get upset, I would be much more upset at the thought that we could never again have a natural, relaxed conversation about the things that are important to us. I do understand that *you* might find it distressing as well, but I really would appreciate it if you tried to talk to me about the things which worry me.' In a similar way, you might like to advise those who attempt to do everything for you, to place you into a child-like, helpless role. You may even wish to say something of this nature before people start to look embarrassed or awkward, to tell them that you understand that they don't know what to say and to make it clear what you would and wouldn't like to talk about.

Of course, you may not be sure yourself how you would like people to react. To some extent you may have to work things out as you go along, talking to a friend and then picking up on those parts of the conversation with which you weren't happy. You may feel awkward telling your friends or relatives how you'd like them to behave — if so, your close ally may be useful here. Friends will often, in any case, feel easier in the initial stages talking to a spouse or other special person. Doing so may give that person the opportunity to point out what kind of behaviour may be most acceptable.

If you are the friend or relative of a dying person, the best single thing you can do is to be scrupulously honest. If you feel awkward, embarrassed or unsure, then say so. Don't try to cover up such feelings by changing the subject, or laughing nervously, or blurting out a flood of apologies. If there are things you feel should be said, but you're not sure what the reaction will be, then ask. Saying something like, 'I'm not sure what I should and shouldn't say to you. I feel that I should avoid anything to do with dying for fear of upsetting you, yet, at the same time, I know that it's important to you and that you might feel better for being able to talk about it. I suppose what I'm saying is I'd like some guidance from you on whether you'd prefer to avoid particular subjects or to feel free to talk about them as and when they arise.'

For all of those involved in such conversations, friends, relatives and the dying themselves, it is important to remember that what can and cannot be talked about may change over time. The level of discussion that's appropriate at one time may have changed a month, a week or even a day later. For everyone concerned, the simple rule is 'when in doubt, be honest and explicit'.

All of which, of course, should be considered in the context of the many other things there are to talk about as well. Although the process of dying is likely to be of overwhelming importance to the person concerned, this is not to say that all interest in other things will instantly fade into insignificance. The dying person will still want to hear news of children, of career plans, of gossip and even of what's been happening in the latest episodes of favourite soap operas! Just as the topic of dying should not be arbitrarily excluded from conversation, so it should not be allowed to take over and monopolize it.

In general, the aim should be to acknowledge that the dying person cannot simply carry on as before, while at the same time remembering that she or he is essentially still the same person. Attempting to do everything for such a person is unwise — the dying person has precious little life left and someone else attempting to take it over will probably receive hostility rather than thanks. Patronizing sympathy is likely to be misplaced; in general, it is not terribly pleasant to lose one's dignity and autonomy, being regarded as simply a 'poor thing'. Rather, what is needed is *empathy*, an attempt to understand how the dying person feels and, as far as possible, to try to share as much as possible of the burden this involves. The most helpful friends are likely to be those who take the trouble to find out what the dying person would actually like them to do, rather than simply imposing their own views of what is best.

Summary

Once the news has been broken that a person has a fatal illness, both the patient and those around them need to go through a process of adaptation. Such adaptation may initially involve a period of denial, where the patient tries to avoid accepting all or part of the situation; a parallel to this may be found in the reaction of some friends and relatives, who may talk of 'miracle' cures. Yet for most people this denial will only be a passing phase. Any or all of the stages described by Kubler-Ross — denial, anger, bargaining, depression and acceptance may be experienced.

For the dying person, this period of adaptation is likely to involve considerable reassessment of one's relationship to one's body. No longer is the body that reliable system which is synonymous with one's sense of self. It may now come to be seen as somehow alien. Even one's thoughts and dreams may be surprising and seem separate. Throughout all this it is important for the dying person to maintain a sense of self, to remember that underneath all the physical changes happening to their body they are still essentially the same person.

For others, too, this may be an essential point to recognize. Although a fatal illness inevitably creates a barrier, it is important to remember that one's dying friend or relative is still the same person. Initially, it is likely that friends or relatives will find it difficult to talk to the dying person, not knowing how to behave. When this happens, talking about what to talk about may help considerably.

During this period, everyone concerned is going to go through changes. Fears, anxieties and uncertainties all have to be coped with. Such a period is never going to be easy, but with good communication, some of the difficulties can at least be reduced.

Practical implications

This chapter has raised many issues which have practical implications for both the dying person and for their friends and relatives. Many of these are also important for those professionally responsible for the care of the dying. Such implications include:

- Trying to understand that part of one's early response to the news that one is dying may be a reluctance to accept some of the information. It's not necessary for the dying person to force such acceptance — it's probably better to allow acceptance to occur naturally.

- The dying person's perception of their body may change, the body being seen as something alien, separate, and negative, that cannot be trusted. At the same time, thoughts and dreams may seem intrusive and often disturbing. This should be accepted as a normal and natural part of adaptation. The maintenance of the dying person's sense of identity is something that can be worked on by everybody.

- One's close ally can be a useful person, with whom issues can be discussed and who can take on tasks which the dying person cannot or would rather not do. Since such an ally will usually be a close loved one, it is important also to discuss in detail with this person the anxieties the dying person has for them.

- During this period of uncertainty, the dying person may seem rather fragile emotionally. This should not be taken as an excuse to 'shield' the person from reality but rather as an indication of the need for extra support in dealing with this reality. In practical terms, this means being willing to talk about disturbing topics and being willing to handle the tears and passing distress that this may cause with empathy and without dismissing them or changing the subject. The dying person should have no qualms at this stage about making full use of external support and resources.

- With acceptance of the situation comes a number of questions about the course of the illness, treatment and so on. Some of these can be answered only very approximately, if at all. The more possible it is to obtain answers, even if they are only vague, the more possible it becomes to reduce uncertainty. This done, the remaining uncertainty may simply have to be accepted.

- Time being limited, it's necessary to think more closely about one's priorities. Again, one's close ally can be a useful person with whom to discuss this.

- Most people have little idea about how to respond to a dying person. The situation creates a barrier between the patient and others. These two factors conspire to make communication difficult and sometimes impossible and some friends may simply stay away. Much of this can be avoided by an early discussion of what is appropriate behaviour. Often, the dying person will be glad of the opportunity to talk about death, or about practical problems. Most dying people prefer *empathy* to *sympathy*.

- Since this is a period of adaptation for everyone, it is important not to assume that immediate reactions are necessarily an indicator of long-term reactions. Acceptance comes at different rates to different people, and the person who seems least able to cope at the beginning may turn out to be the most able later.

4
Getting on with living

In the previous chapter we talked about the early responses to the news that one is dying and how this demands a process of adaptation. In one sense, of course, this will continue for the remainder of the dying person's life. To have a fatal illness brings about a dramatic change in status, with some separateness and isolation from others being inevitable. Nevertheless, for many people there will be a substantial period between hearing the news of their illness and their eventual death. During this period, many of the normal activities of life will continue as before, indeed, it is probably important to the person's maintenance of a sense of self that as many of the old familiar activities and routines as possible *do* continue. A complete and absolute change in every aspect of one's life is only likely to undermine one's self-confidence and sense of identity.

To talk of maintaining normal activities may seem to conflict with what we have said earlier about the impossibility of simply carrying on as before. To pretend that nothing has happened would be unrealistic, but this doesn't mean that *everything* has to change. Rather it is necessary to consider carefully what *must* change and what can carry on as before.

Carrying on with living will inevitably involve giving up some of the things which were previously a normal part of life. Some things will *have* to be given up; other things the dying person may simply *want* to give up. Deciding on what should and shouldn't be given up is not something which is done all at once, nor is it necessarily appropriate to start thinking of such things as soon as one knows that one is dying. As mentioned in chapter 3, the person will usually take some time to absorb the idea, to accept the fact that they are dying, a process which may contunue for a prolonged period. In the early stages of the process of adaptation, the person is likely to be too shocked to give much thought to ways of carrying on. Things may well look so bleak that there seems little point in planning or organizing the future. It may however not be long before the person starts to adapt to the idea and to begin to think more positively, at which stage it is possible to think seriously about planning the future.

Developing a positive outlook: Freda's experience

Within a month or so of her diagnosis Freda began to think that things were starting to settle:

> *I must be getting over the first shock because I'm beginning to fight some things.*

Within six months she noted how this 'beginning to fight' was taking shape in more positive thinking:

> *I realize I am taking some comfort from . . . reasoning . . . as follows: The main problem is the secondaries, probably in the spine. They have responded quite markedly to radiotherapy. I am a lot more agile than ever I was before Christmas.*

Recognizing that treatment is actually having positive results can be a great influence in giving the dying person more hope for the future. For Freda, such a shift towards a more positive approach to her illness was something to discuss with Les:

> *I have a contract with myself not to be frightened by my situation or the future. I was able to explain to Les how I saw it at present. It is as if . . . we, mainly Les and I, have . . . set ourselves high standards for behaviour and attitudes. I may not have the means to do it all, i.e., that it will take more of my inner resources than I have. . . . It seems that I am doing a lot of intellectualizing; I don't think it's useful!*

Similarly, Freda found talking things over with her general practitioner helpful:

> *All his comments have suggested that it is reasonable to feel what I am feeling, in the circumstances. I must say I was fairly relieved to hear that, it has helped throughout these past few days, has helped me to keep saying it.*

and with another doctor:

> *It was a relief to explain how I felt about some things these past few*

days. He offered me some antidepressants because the way I was feeling possibly could be called 'depressed', but I'm certain that I will derive no benefit from them and the doctor agreed! Just to hear him confirm some of the things I am thinking helps, i.e., you have done well, it's understandable in your position. I was at least able to voice, or rather put words to, my worries about the future.

What we see in these comments of Freda's is the benefit of communicating how she felt. Not only does this help the dying person in planning for the future, it also provides an opportunity to reduce uncertainty associated with their position. Knowing that one is dying demands substantial adaption, and it is not surprising that the dying person may experience some anxiety during this period. In Freda's case, she felt some insecurity regarding whether or not her feelings were appropiate; talking to others gave her the reassurance she wanted. It was clear, also, that the communication was welcomed by others.

It's a good thing to communicate how I am feeling — they all said that they would feel bad not knowing how I am feeling.

Remarks like these reflect Freda's keenness to get on with enjoying life again. Sure enough, it wasn't long before her diary entry for the day started, 'I woke with a feeling I *wanted* to get up and get the morning routine in motion.'

With the development of a more positive outlook comes the chance to take stock of the situation. Careful evaluation of the impact of diagnosis and the probable course of the illness will inevitably highlight losses which have resulted from it, either directly or indirectly. Perhaps surprisingly, there are also likely to be gains. Both of these merit closer consideration.

The losses in dying

Many of the losses associated with the knowledge that one is dying are self-evident. There is, even if not loss of *hope* for a long-term future, at least a loss of the *confidence* in such a future. Many of us take for granted the continuity of life almost indefinitely; being forced to confront the issue of our own death may be deeply disturbing.

But as well as these, there are likely to be other losses, physical, psychological and personal. Physically a fatal illness will more often than not involve some degree of pain or discomfort, as Freda soon discovered:

Over the past few days the bone pain . . . has become worse — got stuck on the studio couch today. I am not sure how practical it is to expect the drugs to deal with it all. No real pain anywhere except on movement.

and:

I spent the evening in front of the television. Got rather hot and felt a bit dizzy on getting up.

Coupled with this, both the illness and the treatment may mean that the dying person has much less energy to draw on:

The loss of a 'mainspring' of energy seems to be the thing I miss most at the moment.

Besides these physical problems, there may be a number of psychological problems. We noted earlier in the chapter how Freda often found herself feeling 'depressed', and how helpful she found it to talk to others. Such a feeling may be very oppressive:

It is a very difficult feeling to overcome, a feeling of being very miserable, it seems to go deep down. If you are feeling sorry for yourself, and afraid in any way, it just makes it worse. I can, sometimes, make it pass off by relaxing and thinking positive thoughts.

Such feelings need not be unbeatable:

Felt much better as the day progressed, also with the thought that it is such a waste of time feeling miserable and feeling sorry for myself.

A less obvious psychological problem that can affect the dying person is that of guilt. In general, we like to feel that we have control over our lives, when something bad happens it's hard to resist the thought that this might be the result of our own behaviour. Like other people in similar situations, Freda found herself experiencing such feelings:

Suddenly it came to me — I should have adjusted my life to give me more relaxation — an embarrassing moment. I think, deep down, I still feel guilty that I have cancer — it must be something I have done.

With the knowledge that one has a serious illness comes a considerable amount of worry about the significance of any new symptom. As a doctor, Freda noticed this particularly:

I had been rather concerned by the fact that, just recently, my stomach has been feeling bloated, and have had a feeling of being unable to take a deep breath. I therefore got to wondering if my liver is enlarged. I rang my GP (after thinking about it for a few days), he couldn't feel anything so he has fixed for me to see the specialist. He also thought everything was okay on examination, however I felt a little uneasy, maybe because I have had to consider the possibility 'what happens next?' The specialist remarked, characteristically, 'It's an occupational hazard.' I suppose it's difficult to know what to take note of and what to ignore. I still maintain I am grateful for as much relevant knowledge as I can have, the unknown has far more terrors for me than the known.

The overall effect of these and other worries may be to leave the individual feeling delicate and fragile, with rapid and substantial changes in mood:

I became frustrated at the waiting time . . . I was stiff all the time I was walking around during the afternoon. I felt very tearful and negative. The following day was completely different. I worked on my black and white prints for the club competition next week. I do feel very fragile, thin-skinned.

On top of all this, it may become necessary to cope with the problems of others. Sadly, many people are unable to cope with the dying person, and relationships may deteriorate substantially. People may distance themselves from the dying person, making excuses, substituting cards or flowers for themselves or only maintaining contact through others;

X has not been in touch with us at all, these past months. X wrote directly to Les on first knowing I was ill, as though I was to be bypassed. I know I am supersensitive about it, I could be thought egocentric — I am! So often during the early days . . . people would ring up to speak to Les, or ring when I was not around.

Some may find that the thought of the dying person brings to the fore fears of their own death, especially with older people. Many may change dramatically in their manner, becoming condescending or patronizing, talking to the dying person as they would talk to a child. Freda wondered if such a strategy was simply a convenient way of formalizing a difficult relationship — with the added problem that she noticed herself sometimes pandering to this expectation, adopting a child-like frame of mind!

Relationships with others need not always, however, deteriorate. Sometimes careful communication may help others to cope. Each person has their own way of dealing with what Freda came to call her 'illness task'. Freda sometimes found it necessary to explain her own behaviour.

> . . . *to try to help her understand why I have gone about this 'illness task' as I have, my feelings about the rest of my life up to it, etc. I will have to put it into words because if I succeed she will begin to understand and will feel closer — rather than drifting apart . . . maybe she became frightened by the show of strength I put on at the beginning — I know from experience that when someone shows strength in these circumstances it separates you if you cannot possibly see how the person can do this, it makes you break off in fright.*

Not all relationships will change for the worse. Indeed, the knowledge that a person is dying can enhance some relationships:

> *As time passed, relationships grew with various friends and relatives who were able to give valuable support and I learned how to make use of these for everyone's benefit.*

These improvements to relationships that dying can bring leads us to one of the more paradoxical of issues — the fact that dying, besides involving losses, may also involve a number of gains. If the future is to be planned effectively, these gains need to be considered in conjunction with the inevitable losses.

Gains in dying

To suggest that there are gains to be had from dying is not, of course, to say that dying is a good thing. Nonetheless, it would be unrealistic and untruthful to suggest that there are *no* positive aspects in being a dying person. For Freda, some of these benefits were very tangible. One of the first ways in which she took advantage of the fact that she was dying came from a discussion we had at an early point. Having talked around the rather unsatisfactory communications she had experienced, she resolved to make a positive contribution to the future training of professionals by making a videotape aimed at exploring communication in terminal care. She was, of course, already deeply involved in organizing local training courses for general practitioners, and was well aware of the gaps that existed in their training. She discussed the matter with a number of her colleagues involved in training and concluded, 'I am so sure the tape is a good idea that I talked it into existence.' Indeed she did, for with the help of the Liverpool University Communications Studies Department, and sponsorship from Napp Laboratories to cover costs of producing the tape and accompanying booklet the project was completed and well received by its users:

> *The following week was the Course Organizers' Conference . . . so I took the opportunity to send the tape so that it will become as widely used as possible. I had already written to the organizer of the conference explaining what it was all about. He replied, almost by return of post, expressing interest. It was shown in an optional 'slot' in the timetable. About forty — half of the delegates — saw it.*

The interest generated by the video led to Freda being involved in speaking to a number of professional groups about the topic of death and dying, experiences which she found particularly fulfilling:

> *A real red letter day when I spoke on communication in terminal care at the college's annual research symposium. It helped a lot to know the content of what I said had arisen out of my own experience and so it was truly mine.*

Similarly keeping her diaries and various articles and this book were activities which produced a great deal of satisfaction, even though she was, sadly, unable to live to see this book's actual production:

> *I feel I have been very fortunate to share my diaries with Les and the girls, so that in a way we feel there is some purpose in it . . . it has been very therapeutic.*

Benefits like these are largely a function of Freda's substantial involvement with the teaching of other doctors. Few people who are dying will have the expertise, resources or opportunity to do anything similar. For most people, the benefits will be less tangible even if no less important. Going for a short walk to the village, about a year into her illness, Freda realized:

> *I am seeing the world almost through a child's eyes. The details of the countryside, clumps of primroses and violets, the shape of wild garlic flowers, the shape and colour of the newly opened ash branches give me great pleasure.*

She found other perceptions enhanced as well, for example, when she went to a concert she remarked:

> *I was immediately drawn in to the spirit of the music. It is as though*

these days there are no distractions to listening and I am able to receive the music at a different, more real level.

Not only were her own perceptions of the world around her affected, so were her perceptions of herself:

I have had experiences which I never would have had, for which I have to thank the cancer. Humility, coming to terms with my own mortality, knowledge of my inner strength which continually surprises me, and more things about myself which I have discovered, because I have had to stop in my tracks, reassess and proceed. I would have found the increasing disability due to old age very hard to bear.

In all, there may turn out to be occasions when the status of the dying person leads to a greater appreciation of the positive things in life, as Freda noted on holiday a year or so after her diagnosis:

I am enjoying being lazy. I don't have to do anything I don't want to. I am beginning to enjoy life as I used to, so much the sweeter by contrast.

During the time she was dying Freda noted many such gains from her situation. Some gains she felt could be used justifiably — for example, the authority her experience gave her when passing an opinion on the subject of dying. This, she felt, could be used for good, rather than for her own gratification. Other gains offered temptations which were perhaps less justifiable. She recognized, for example, the power of being an invalid, of being able to ask people to do things for you:

I made it a rule at the beginning of my illness, to do as much as I can for myself, to try not to ask anyone to do anything for me that I can do for myself.

As a working rule, Freda's is one which certainly resists the temptation simply to give up, to resign oneself to a 'sick' role. In some respects however it might be a little more strict than most of us would like — indeed, how many people who are *not* dying could live up to such a rule? Possibly a more workable rule for most people would be 'not to ask anyone to do anything for me that I can do for myself unless I'd have asked them to do the same when I was not ill'. It is certainly worth recognizing how tempting it can be simply to resign oneself to being an invalid. Setting up a rule something like Freda's can help prevent oneself from giving in completely.

We can see that, besides the losses associated with dying,

Freda was able to identify specific gains. Although we have discussed these separately, the losses, gains and the development of a positive attitude are all closely linked. Indeed, over time, it's likely that the person will continue to identify different losses and gains, all of which will influence the ability to think positively. In the same way, the plans and strategies for the future will change and adapt over time.

Thus, with more positive thinking, and a recognition of both losses and gains, it became possible for Freda to set about organizing the process of getting on with living.

Getting on with living

During this phase of her illness, Freda came to recognize the need to plan out what future she had, to recognize what she could and couldn't do, what she wanted and didn't want to do, and to approach things constructively:

Once the shock of the bad news has settled, a period of mental stock-taking takes place and one is left in a situation which is slightly different to how it first appeared to be. The thinking goes, 'everyone has to die sometime — is it very much different from the inevitable growing old phase of everyone's life?'

The difference is in its speed of action, the unpleasant shock of hearing one has a fatal illness speeds the adjustment to the situation — if one was unable to respond positively, the burden would overtake one's life and one would be submerged and paralysed by grief and the weight of it.

For me the situation became a challenge, a new way of living, time scale changed. There were many things it would not be possible to do again, but, in concentrating my mind, priorities emerged.

Some hobbies had to be tested out, because some, like fell-walking or energetic cycling, were limited by my physical condition. In photography, however, I was able to exploit my growing tolerance and patience with inanimate objects.

It is necessary to be quite matter of fact and disciplined about how I spend my time.

Much of Freda's normal lifestyle could be retrieved fairly straightforwardly. She had already obtained a year's leave to attend a clinical psychology training course. She joined this and soon described herself as 'becoming at home'. She returned to her hobby of photography, and within a short time was looking positively towards the future:

The evening was spent putting final touches to the camera club entry
for the competition. I enjoyed competing, as I had black and white,
colour prints and slides. The black and white won in the beginners'
section and I do hope to produce many more, and better prints next
season.

Freda's look to the future was prophetic; later in the year she
won the camera club's advanced colour slide trophy! In her diary
she commented 'It does give me such a boost to succeed in
photography.' Her proudest achievement came when she discovered that she had won the camera club vase for the best
performance in competition throughout the year. I visited her the
following morning, when she told me that the first thing she had
thought on awakening that day was, 'I've won the Club Vase!'

For Freda, getting on with the business of living was disrupted
by a stroke which she suffered early on in her treatment. The
stroke had a number of effects including some disruption of her
speech, causing her a great deal of distress. Nevertheless, her
symptoms began to improve within a fairly short time, and by
three months after the stroke she wrote:

I am finding it is easier to go out in the evenings now, I feel more
sociable than before, conversation is not such a strain. It would be
appropriate to comment on my speech, right now. Usually fairly
fluent throughout the day, I occasionally substitute he for she or miss
a word completely. The worst times are when I need to be more
emphatic, more formal or when I am upset or tense. It becomes a
vicious circle.

Important in settling down to getting on with living is the
recognition of any progress in treatment. Such progress was used
early on by Freda to adjust her expectations of what she should
and shouldn't be able to do:

As we walked Les remarked that, as I was walking a lot quicker than
before, perhaps it would be a good idea to include a proper walk in my
daily routine. I am realizing that the numb, rather odd, feelings in
my legs and feet are not very noticeable these days. I am getting
steadier too. Apart from some aching in my neck and ocasional prickly
feelings on bending my neck, my spine symptoms have receded almost
completely.

And soon afterwards:

I am steadily getting on with living. I have had to learn to slow down
— my thoughts and actions, and to control my temper — I haven't

the energy to lose my temper . . . I do wish I had known about all this long ago!

When organizing the business of living it is clearly important to recognize that any plans will need to be flexible, and able to be adapted according to the way the illness develops. Freda found she needed to increase and decrease different parts of her activity in the light of her changing feelings.

On learning that one is dying, there may well be an intuitive feeling that life can never again be fully enjoyable, that the shadow of death hanging over the person will cloud any enjoyment. In this light, it is worth looking at some of Freda's writings in the period following her diagnosis:

Today has been one of the best days I can remember. It was brilliant sunshine, blue skies, white woolly clouds. We are going ahead with filling many rolls of film — using a filter for the clouds on black and white. There are a few good viewpoints on the way down Troutbeck to Ambleside. (Written during a stay in the Lake District.)

And:

Yesterday should have been a short book of its own because, from start to finish, it was a perfect day. Bright sunshine tempted us to go straight out with our cameras, as soon as we had finished our breakfast. The grass had a silvery appearance from the dew, it was close to frost. When we realized the sun was still climbing up behind the hills across the valley, we went up Robin Lane behind the village Post Office. We were looking for some interesting rooftops for the next camera club competition. As we reached the top and were looking down to Lake Windermere, we came across a sort of magic scene. The mist still hung over the lake and the side valleys, the sun above it made it appear very white and thick, most photogenic. (Written some four months later, also in the Lake District.)

Not that it was necessary to go away for days like that:

Yesterday was one of the best days I have had for some time, beautiful start, went off to Sefton Park. Again, today has been a day to remember, our good weather continues . . . we had lunch in the garden, joy of joys a pair of goldfinches visited us. There was a flash of colour: red, white and yellow and a flutter of wings — there they were on the little apple tree by the pond. Thirty seconds and they were away. (Written about five weeks before Freda's death.)

Days like these demonstrate clearly the fact that to be told that one is dying need not prevent one from going on living. Freda herself was very concerned that people in her situation should be able to learn this from her:

> *I want people to know that there is a fair streak of 'teacher' in me, this is one big spur for progress in writing and lecturing. I feel as though I may be entering a different, more mature phase of acceptance . . . I am beginning to balance my losses and gains more realistically. I have really enjoyed this week, or rather, this spell of rest, listening to music, doing photography, writing letters and generally learning to live more.*

Learning from Freda's experience

Obviously, each person in a situation like Freda's will have to develop a personal approach to getting on with the business of living. However, it's worth stepping back a little from Freda's experiences and looking at the lessons that can be learned.

At a most general level, going forward requires that the person learns to think positively, identifying both the gains and losses of the situation, and adapting accordingly. For most people, as it was for Freda, the ease with which they can start looking to the future is likely to depend, at least to some extent, on the availability of support from others. An important aspect of this is ensuring that these others are aware of how the dying person feels. We saw earlier how Freda was reassured by telling others how she felt. Once again, we see the benefits of having a 'special' person with whom feelings, worries, anxieties, can be discussed.

We've already noted, however, that other people may be unsure of how to behave. Since the reaction of others can be of considerable importance, it's perhaps worth identifying a few general guidelines. Openness and a willingness to listen to what the dying person has to say are likely to be of critical importance. Attempting to avoid the subject of the person's illness is only going to deny the reality of their experience. As Freda put it, when she was told that someone was nervous about seeing her:

> *I reacted rather quickly and said, 'I won't bite.' I wouldn't be me if I didn't make the point that cancer is something to be brought out into the open, to be talked about freely.*

Often the person who's unsure how to behave will go over the top in trying to do things for someone who's dying. But rather than fussing and creating an artificial situation, there may be a lot to be gained from simply getting on with normal activities.

Freda's husband Les, for example, made a deliberate decision to continue with his photographic work being prepared for submission to the Royal Photographic Society for his Associateship award. The day his submission was passed was, for Freda, another 'real red-letter day'. Similarly she was pleased when Madeleine, who was going out running regularly, discussed it with her.

> *A few weeks ago she [Madeleine] asked me if I minded her going running. I suppose that could have been rephrased, 'Are you jealous?' I was touched and said, 'Well, you are running for me now, aren't you?' So we are doing well.*

Remember that amongst the distressing emotions which may be felt at this time is guilt. If it appears that the illness is causing total disruption of the lives of one's family and friends, the dying person may end up feeling guilty, not just about dying, but also the fact that they're still living.

In terms of planning the future, much of this will have to be on a week-by-week, month-by-month basis. Often this may mean having to give up or miss things, with associated disappointment:

> *I had planned to go to a psychology meeting in Manchester on the whole subject of psychological problems in cancer patients. I am obviously very much interested in it, but sometimes I must cut my losses.*

At all times, however, it's important to maintain hope of improvement again where this is possible:

> *Since I last wrote I have become calmer, more helpful, almost manic . . . I want to continue my life as it was before it was so suddenly broken last October, so that the sense of loss is diminshed. In the early days, I looked at the pictures of beaches on television and envied those who were there. When we first went to the Lake District, I felt quite separate from the hikers who walked everywhere so quickly. Now I can walk quickly, bend down, turn around, roll over in bed, sleep on my side.*

Sometimes taking up things from where they left off can be both rewarding and unnerving, as when Freda returned to work after the year's psychology course:

> *Back to work! It should have been a red-letter day in terms of positive thinking. However, it went very smoothly. Many of my regulars know I was back and seemed glad to see me. The 'should' above was because of feelings of anxiety, will I be able to cope? Will I be able to*

finish in time to get enough rest? These thoughts are counter-productive and restrictive. They stem from my loss of confidence.

Often tiredness will be a problem, and here a systematic structuring of the daily routine may help the person to do more:

I am feeling gradually more confident, more used to the restricted peace, physical and mental. One big help has been my rather rigid routine – I am upset by changes in schedule and like to have everything planned out. Perhaps this is a fault, but it seems to be working and it helps me to achieve things; writing, phone calls and so on.

Commonly, either the illness or its treatment will involve losses which can be predicted and it will often be tempting to avoid thinking about these things until they occur. This is not always the best way to react. More often than not, it will be better to anticipate as much as possible so that the dying person is prepared for the loss and has had time to adjust to the idea. Such planning may include considering the choosing of a wig if treatment is to lead to hair loss, arranging for the availability of a wheelchair if loss of mobility is expected and so on.

Most importantly, however, the dying person should determine to continue with those activities which are possible and enjoyable, fighting the temptation to give up completely. By acknowledging limitations, and evaluating gains, it is possible to return to many of the activities of everyday life.

Summary

Even when dying, it's necessary to get on with living. After the initial shock and adaptation to the news that one is dying, a shift towards more positive thinking becomes possible. At this stage, it's possible to take stock of the gains and losses and to plan the future accordingly. Losses — physical, psychological and personal — will inevitably impose some limitations on what can be done. By contrast, the gains in dying may open up opportunities which hadn't been there previously (Freda's professional work on the subject of dying) or may enhance existing hobbies and pastimes (Freda's increased appreciation of music and nature). It is important to recognize the role of the people around you in this. Some people may find dealing with someone who is dying difficult, making careful communication necessary. Other relationships may be enhanced. By bringing fears and anxieties out into the open they can be confronted and frequently resolved. With such obstacles removed, everyone can collaborate in working out solutions to difficulties, with the result that the person who is dying can, nevertheless, experience happiness in living.

Practical implications

The topics we've considered in this chapter have many implications for those concerned with dying. If the dying person is to make the most of their life, careful consideration of practicalities is important. Such practicalities include:

- Once the initial shock is over, and more positive thinking is beginning is probably a good time to start working out what changes will be necessary. This is not to say that the dying person should be pressurized into thinking positively. In most cases it's probably better to let people get over the shock in their own good time. Often a positive attitude will develop as the person begins to notice improvements with treatment.

- Losses brought about by the change in one's life expectancy need to be faced and considered realistically. If it looks as though some enjoyable activities will no longer be possible, then this has to be accepted. If benefits in the treatment or progress of the illness make them possible again, all well and good, but, in the meantime, life must go on. Nine times out of ten, there will still be many enjoyable activities and pastimes which can be pursued.

- Similarly, the gains involved in dying should be acknowledged. Sometimes it will be possible, as it was for Freda, to make use of the fact that one is dying. If this is not possible there are likely to be other gains. Some of these will enhance areas of life while others may provide temptations which need to be resisted, as Freda did with her rule about not asking others to do things.

- The dying person's emotional response may be complex, and discussing this with others may provide considerable reassurances. Simply to be told that it is reasonable to feel anxious, depressed and so on may be a great help. The dying person may feel guilty about being ill at all and such a reaction may be difficult to talk about, particularly if there *is* reason to implicate the person in their own illness (as when a smoker contracts lung cancer). Talking about the issues enables them to be put in perspective. Like most feelings of guilt, not talking about them is likely to make them worse, whilst bringing them out into the open may eliminate them completely.

- Similarly, the reactions of others may be highly variable. If you are dying, and you feel that someone is finding your situation difficult to cope with, don't try to avoid the subject with the intention of making them feel better —more often than not this will simply perpetuate the whole problem. Far better to bring the subject out into the open, and explain to others why you're reacting in the way you are.

- Face up to practical difficulties, prepare for them if possible, and work out ways around them if you can. If you find yourself tired a lot of the time, for example, identify which things tire you most and ask yourself honestly whether it's worth continuing to do them. Remember that a routine and a structure can make activities less tiring, so, if you're tired, get into the habit of setting aside particular times of day for seeing people, going out, writing letters, taking a nap, etc.

- If the dying person is a friend or member of your family, beware the temptation to make a fuss and do everything for them. Living is about doing things for ourselves, and simply to be fussed over and cosseted is more likely to make the person feel worse. By all means, do things which would be distressing or impossible for the dying person to do. But avoid taking over their lives and taking away their autonomy. The person who is dying is likely to be struggling to maintain a sense of self and a personal identity, something which is difficult if one's whole lifestyle and interactions with others are changed. Remember also that people will feel guilty if others are being put to any trouble; the dying person may aleady feel guilty about dying; don't make them guilty about living.

- Similarly, don't immediately give up all the things you find enjoyable in order to devote yourself nobly to your loved one's last days. Far from making the dying person feel loved, it's much more likely to make them feel a nuisance. Remember that if there are things you enjoy, then your loved one, even when dying, may be able to share that enjoyment through you.

- Above all, don't run away from the dying person. Cards and flowers are nice, but as an addition to personal contact, not as a substitute for it.

- Finally, remember that the news that one is dying doesn't mean that life will never again be enjoyable. Even in this new situation, it's still possible to experience 'a perfect day'.

5
Dealing with problems

In the previous chapter we discussed the need to balance an awareness of dying with getting on with living. In practice, though, this will often seem difficult as various problems occur.

In one sense, some of the problems which are likely to arise have already been discussed under the heading of losses in dying. The illness itself is likely to give rise to a number of problems such as pain, tiredness, uncertainty, loneliness and a general feeling of being fragile and thin-skinned:

> *One morning in Newcastle, when I woke, I seemed to have quite a lot of pain in my neck and also my back. Suddenly I felt hopeless and panicky.*

Such problems may make the person more irritable for a while:

> *I am becoming irritated with a few little things, filing not up to date, path. lab. reports not left out for me. I suppose it's nothing new, but I have not the energy to assert myself effectively.*

The bad feelings from the illness may end up being taken out on those who are closest:

> *Being exhausted and very depressed last evening led to one of these very stressful wrangles with Les in which we argued in circles as to whether or not I should have worked that day! What a waste of time — we are in complete agreement anyway.*

When this happens, it's important to remember that irritability with others is quite normal now and then. There's a serious risk that when some sort of argument happens, everybody will end up feeling guilty. It's better if, following such an argument, you take the opportunity to talk it through and learn from the experience.

The treatment prescribed for the illness may itself cause

serious difficulties; Freda's stroke, for example, may have been related to her treatment. It certainly presented as a major problem:

> *I can't describe my awakening this morning, I gather it was quite dramatic . . . I saw I was puzzled by a rather strange-looking hand lying on my left side — it didn't feel like my own. There was Les trying to move me around in the bed and trying to get me moved. He was making calls to the doctor. 'Freda's all gone floppy.' The doctor came round. I realized I had difficulty understanding spoken words. I had difficulty in swallowing, my mouth was so dry. I went to the hospital by ambulance, Les following in the car.*

Of course, treatment doesn't always have such drastic side-effects. Other, less damaging, but still distressing problems may occur, such as hair loss and nausea associated with chemotherapy, and even just the inconvenience of travelling for treatment.

On top of the problems associated with the illness are those which are caused by other illnesses. Just as the normally healthy person will fall victim to the occasional cold or bout of 'flu, so will the person with a serious illness. Where, however, the normally healthy person will take such an illness as a matter of course, the seriously ill person may be hit particularly hard. Not only does such an illness use up some of the precious remaining days of life, it also generates particular fears, as Freda discovered:

> *I have had the misfortune to be struck down by a 'flu-like cold — Les had it last weekend. I was hoping — as usual — to pass it by. By yesterday, I was near to packing up completely. For the first time in my illness I did not want to get up.*

Moreover, such fears are not necessarily overcome just by being logical:

> *Logic says the cold is running its normal course, but it feels different, my bone pains are getting worse — difficult to assess at the best of times — but always stiff after rest, I am waking in pain most days . . . I became alarmed that this cold would finish me off.*

These and similar problems will also give rise to other difficulties not directly related to the illness. Impairment of functioning may, for example, lead to a reduced mobility, with consequent restriction in activity. Opportunities may be missed, and normal activities like work may have to be given up. And of course, as we saw in chapter 4, there may be the problem of dealing with the difficulties other people have in relating to the person who is ill.

> *I was right in thinking that they are very ill at ease with me, very frightened but, despite the awkwardness, I was very glad indeed to see them.*

Inevitably, the problems that arise will be specific to each individual to some extent. Two people may be quite similar, with similar illnesses, yet the problems they encounter may be completely different. Not all the problems will be soluble. Nevertheless it is helpful to consider some of the general strategies and tactics which may be adopted in coping with problems and setbacks.

Dealing with problems

It may seem like stating the obvious, but a useful first step in dealing with problems is to recognize them. Nevertheless, identification of a problem may take a surprising time. It was some fifteen months after her diagnosis, for example, before Freda recognized explicitly how important emotional control was to her:

> *I wish I could deal with my emotions better. I suppose that's the secret of my survival in my present circumstances.*

Problems can often be anticipated, although, even when this is possible, the actual confrontation with them can still be distressing. For example, Freda had known for some time that her illness made it impractical for her to carry on driving a car, but when the letter came confirming this it was still a shock:

> *Saturdays's post brought a letter from the Driver and Vehicle Licensing Centre in Swansea saying that my licence is to be withdrawn. It was a shock seeing it in black and white, I thought I had accepted it. During that day I experienced what has since been described to me as acute depression, the feeling of dragging down was quite a real pain. I felt I had a weight on my chest. I thought I had felt depressed at various times in my lifetime but never so acutely and painfully as this.*

In this instance of course, knowing that the licence was to be withdrawn didn't actually provide Freda with any opportunity to prevent it happening. That is to say, being forewarned still left her helpless. With most problems, the ability to anticipate them will provide the opportunity either to prevent them happening or at least to minimize their impact.

With recognition of problems comes the need and the opportunity to set priorities and realistic aims and limits. Since the time left is, at least to some degree limited, it becomes important for the person who is ill to have some ideas about what things and activities are most important and what less so.

It takes this week's experience to make me realize that I must put myself and my family first, and stop trying to do everything for everybody, over and above my capabilities at the time.

Accepting the limitations imposed by the illness means that the person can concentrate on those activities and priorities which are both achievable and important. Sometimes this may mean, for a while at least, that very limited targets have to be set. After her stroke, for example, Freda found it necessary to pick up her old activities *very* gradually:

I started reading slowly since my stroke, because my concentration was poor. I lost my place and found the place with difficulty.

Even when she had recovered from her stroke, Freda still found it necessary to pay some attention to her limits and priorities:

I . . . need to be in the mood for things. I am becoming used to finding the right time for thinking, reading, doing all sorts of things. In many ways I am becoming wise in choices about my activities, about my companions.

Simply paying attention to these issues may be a source of benefit:

The past week has all been progress. I am learning to pace myself in my work and have some spare energy for other activities.

Usually, however, recognizing the problem and adjusting one's limits and priorities is not enough. Taken to extremes, the result may simply be that the person gives up any activity which becomes difficult. In general, it is preferable if a range of coping strategies can be developed to help to deal with problems either before or when they arise. A number of such strategies can be identified, most of which can be conveniently divided into active and passive methods.

Active coping

Strategies for active coping involve the individual taking some action directly aimed at reducing or solving their problem. One of the most obvious strategies is asking for help and support from others. Many of us feel a little inhibited about asking for help from other people: either we are worried that we seem weak and incapable, or maybe we just don't like to impose on others. If such feelings inhibit you from asking for help, think about how it would feel if someone asked you. The chances are that you'd feel perhaps a little flattered that your friend had chosen *you* to turn to, together with some pleasure at being a help to a person in need. You'd probably be very unlikely to think any the worse of the person for approaching you. And of course, if it's you that needs help, this is the way your friends are likely to think. Certainly Freda's experience was that turning to others could be a tremendous help:

> *How can I sum up the feelings and difficulties that have come my way this week? I have thought hard about it all, because I had not really expected to be hampered by any problems. Perhaps I have let my natural optimism or perhaps it could have been a bit of vanity — I can't let this get me down — get the better of me. So much for this sentiment. More and more, as the days have passed, I have been aware of great feelings of personal loss, I presume because of the damage in the brain [from the stroke] and there is an intellectual gap. It is understandable, but unpleasant to cope with because I don't feel like me!*
>
> *I felt it would be a relief to explain how I am feeling to anyone I thought would understand. Therefore I rang the Director of the Clinical Psychology Course . . . the relief of me telling him was very tangible.*

Freda also took full advantage of the professional help available from the Health Service, consulting a psychiatrist when experiencing particular difficulty, again with good results:

> *Les and I had a long talk with the doctor. We told him how I felt, very weepy and had swings of mood. Eventually he suggested that I see a psychiatrist mainly to advise on medication. I feel I am unable to prescribe for myself and decide on a course of action now. It seems as though I am running out of resources.*
>
> *I went to see the psychiatrist, he was very gentle and fairly laid back. We explored quite a bit about my reactions to other people's reception of the news of my illness.*

And later:

I have just seen the psychiatrist again. He thought I was much better. He was interested in how I coped with knowing I have cancer, and all it implies to me as a doctor. I told him that I thought the improvement in my physical condition was due to a combination of my physical treatment, my attitude and the support of those around me. That was how I saw it, these things were interdependent.

And of course, most importantly, Freda was able to obtain support from her family:

I began to feel very sad and weepy, I talked and talked to Les. I was wallowing, almost enjoying the release of sadness. He is so very good for me, he's just there, comforts me.

Active coping, however, needn't depend on the presence and support of other people. Simply changing one's style of thinking can make a significant difference to the impact of some problems. Adopting a more positive approach to thinking can either help to solve a problem, or at least put it into perspective:

I am beginning to feel that I am overcoming the feelings of isolation and general low-spiritedness . . . My mood is basically unchanged in that despair and panic are never far away . . . but I can state quite firmly my growing conviction, to go on, putting some effort into things that may be difficult . . . There are many moments of relief, of comfort and of hope to compensate.

Of course, it's one thing to talk glibly about 'positive thinking' and another thing actually to be able to do this. In discussing this, Freda used a metaphor of a swimmer in a strong sea. Like the dying person overwhelmed by the situation, the swimmer risks being overwhelmed by the waves. But the swimmer who learns to float is actually buoyed up by the very thing that threatens, just as the dying person who can learn to rise above the distressing thoughts can then be sustained by more positive thinking. As with most problems, the first step is to recognize that they're there:

These past few days I really have felt I am learning to overcome gloomy, counterproductive thoughts and turn them into positive ones. Yesterday afternoon went to bed rather tired, but woke very refreshed after dealing with an attack of miseries.

Converting negative thoughts to positive ones can be done in a number of ways, depending on the problem concerned. Among the ways of converting negative to positive thinking we may include:

Concentrate on progress

When things are getting better, enjoy it. Evidence of this is apparent on a number of occasions in Freda's diaries:

Looking back on the past year it has been all progress apart from the stroke in January. I am continually learning and confirming some very valuable things, as though I am living in reality for the first time ever. I often underestimate what I can do, I usually say of something I have been rather afraid of, 'That was easier than I thought . . .'

I am gradually recovering my strength. I am conscious of great reserves of internal resources. In other words I am becoming the real me, the best me, again . . .

Day by day, inch by inch, I am getting stronger in all ways . . .

Quite a lot of improvement. The pain in my right hip and neck have completely disappeared today . . . also nausea and vomiting much improved.

And:

Life is full of contrasts, and today it is so good to feel the energy and life returning to my body and to my spirits.

Concentrate on what's good, not what's bad

A similar strategy, which will often overlap with the previous one, is to concentrate on the things you *can* do, rather than the things you can't. Rather than paying attention to what's been lost, make the most of the good things you still have:

I left feeling relaxed and that I have been with people who valued and loved me. (After a social gathering.)

This past week, since I returned from Bath, has been full of good things. I am sleeping better (without sedatives), eating more, weight keeps going up . . .

Things are going better and better. I am settling into work . . .

Yesterday was a good day, a team meeting after surgery. I am beginning to feel much more involved . . .

I do get some quick flashes of encouragement which help. On one occasion, on holiday in Lanzarote when I was feeling quite morbid, it suddenly came to me how fortunate I was to be there. I nearly didn't make it, and I experienced a wonderful feeling of being 'glad to be alive' . . .

Today, I felt much more buoyant, more able to talk about my feelings, how I am able to look back over the past weeks and months and see how I have improved, how I have changed. In fact, I have had more real 'boosts' recently than for a long time — real 'glad to be alive' feelings.

Emphasize transience

Many of the problems are things which will, often in a relatively short time, pass away. Sometimes this can have a dramatic effect:

The past week has been very good on the whole, despite it being a 'treatment' week. I have not felt the usual grottiness, except Tuesday afternoon when I suddenly decided it would pass, got up from where I was sitting, and walked about. It passed!

Even if not so dramatic, the changes in a relatively short time may be very definite.

It's a beautiful day, and my feelings of loneliness and drifting which were strong a few days ago, when Easter was finished and normal life began, have dispersed like the lifting of a depression. It is now Thursday. In the last few days things have got better rather than worse, my days are more structured and I generally feel more fulfilled.

This strategy isn't necessarily always easy to apply, but determination can pay off, as two entries from Freda's diaries, a couple of days apart, reveal:

During the night I had a lot of aching and stiffness . . . should be glad to think that the chances are that it will let up sometime in the near future. When I work it out it's never severe and prolonged in the same place. Must remember. (Thursday.)

And:

Saturday passed, a good example of the situation referred to on Thursday. Must practise that philosophy.

Make the most of the present

Dwelling on insoluble problems ahead is unproductive. In some ways the converse of the previous strategy, making the most of the present may be of great value in dealing with anxieties for the future:

I suppose the essence of the pleasure is in the present, neither looking back with regret or nostalgia, nor in looking to the future, certainly not with apprehension and anxiety . . .

Perhaps I have never, in all my life, learned to enjoy the present, be content with what I now experience, because my anxiety about, and lack of confidence in, my future mars the present . . . If I can stand back and consider my present situation, I really have no insurmountable problems.

Convert bad thoughts to good ones

When treatment, in particular, causes difficulties, it may be possible to remember the gains it will bring:

I am becoming more confident of my analgesics — I will *be able to do the little things in life — getting in and out of bed, walking a few steps . . . the price to pay for this at present is a tendency to vomiting, sometimes I need injections.* (Written during Freda's final stay in hospital.)

Don't let a setback take on an importance beyond its true seriousness

I have a superficially thrombosed [blocked] vein on the back of my right hand. No worry, I'll just have to find a different vein next time.

Similarly, when confronted with periods of insomnia:

As I write this, at 4 a.m., I am doing what Les has suggested — if you can't sleep you might as well do something useful.

By learning to think positively like this, it may be possible to reduce the distress caused by the various problems and setbacks which arise. With a little practice at approaching problems positively, it becomes possible for the dying person's confidence to be substantially increased:

. . . thought for the day emerges: there is only one direction to go in — forward, go on living in the same general way — I mean to tackle the difficulties as I have been doing so far.

Besides seeking support and developing strategies of positive thinking, various other tactics can be adopted as means of active coping. Restructuring the physical and social environment can be particularly important here. Following her stroke, for example, Freda sought out the opportunity to spend time away from the hospital and back at home:

I began talking to the staff to ask if I could be allowed home for Saturday and Sunday nights, they think it might be possible. The doctor popped in and gave his permission for the leave. I don't foresee any real problems, only the benefits of being in my own home again.

Conversely, when she recognized the strain of looking after her during her chemotherapy, she took the opposite course and decided to go into hospital:

It was a great relief that I will be admitted to hospital for two nights when I am next given chemotherapy. I noted the relief to be in a safe environment, I'm sure it's a wise move for everyone concerned. It puts the onus on Les to look after me more than is reasonable. He has remarked more than once that he thought he had allowed me to become dehydrated when I was vomiting. I do hope I was able to reassure him.

In a lesser way, minor adjustments to the layout of rooms, etc., can help reduce the distress experienced:

Set up my 'stall' at bed time — bowls, large tissues at the right side of the bed so that there is no chance of vomiting over the side of the bowl. I am learning fiddling little details but they work and make life more comfortable.

With social and interpersonal difficulties direct attack on the problem can also be beneficial, as when Freda talked with members of her clinical psychology course about how she was feeling:

It's a good thing to communicate how I am feeling — they all felt they would feel bad not knowing how I am.

This may be particularly important when dealing with the tension and irritability which leads to difficulties with loved ones:

Because the tension had been building up and I got very worked up, the vicious circle being set up so that I felt I couldn't express myself and became very thin-skinned, wouldn't be comforted. I went at it all with Les, with the resulting build up of tension. It was nice making up and I woke the next morning feeling as though the world was a different place.

Talking to others about how one is feeling can, of course, do much to ease feelings of loneliness. To some extent, this can also be helped by indirectly sharing experiences with others, for example, reading books like this one which talk about people's experience of dying.

Often, of course, physical activity can provide a means of dealing with certain problems:

> *During the past week the pain has gradually improved ... One possible factor in the improvement was going swimming in the University pool ... it was very warm. I stood underneath the hot shower and felt very relaxed.*

As a final thought on active coping, it's worth remembering that little things can often be enough to cheer us up. Many of us have things which we do less often than we'd like and some self-indulgence may do no harm and provide a great deal of pleasure:

> *I wore my best Liberty outfit, I might as well wear it for most occasions when I can.*

Passive coping

It's possible to supplement the active strategies described above with more passive approaches. In particular, learning to relax is a useful skill when dealing with the tensions and anxieties which inevitably arise. Detailed instructions on how to relax are of course more than we have space for in this book. Instructions on relaxation can however be found in a number of books, and it is possible to obtain audio cassettes of instructions to play whilst practising. However, for many people even the basic skills of relaxing a little may be of considerable help. In doing so, a number of points are worth remembering. Firstly, relaxing is a skill, and, like any skill, it takes continued practice for best performance — so don't expect to be able to relax completely at your first attempt. Secondly, it's important to make sure that time is set aside specifically to relax, especially when the skills of deep relaxation are first being learned. Thirdly, it's important to make a distinction between the idea of 'doing something to relax' and actual physical relaxation; many people, for example, describe playing golf as a means of relaxation. What they really mean is that it takes them away from their normal stresses, however, it doesn't involve the total physical and mental relaxation that we're talking about here.

To start learning to relax you should find somewhere where you won't be disturbed and where you can sit or lie comfortably with as little background noise as possible. Take up a comfortable position, close your eyes, and picture a scene of quiet relaxation, for example, lying on a sunny beach, the sound of the waves in the distance and the sun gently warming your body. Try to moderate your breathing so that it becomes deep, slow and rhythmic. Pay attention to the state of your body, noticing any physical tension in your muscles and trying to relax them. If this is difficult it can help if you make the muscle really tense and then suddenly let the tension go. Try to imagine your body is really heavy, that your eyelids are too heavy for you to open them, that your arms and legs are too heavy to move. Enjoy the sensation. Over time, if you practise, you'll find that it becomes easier and easier to drop into a state of total relaxation.

Apart from the physical benefits of relaxation, of course, there is the additional benefit of being distracted from a particular problem. Such distraction itself provides a further passive coping strategy. For Freda, activities such as photography were of great help:

I was stiff all the time I was walking around during the afternoon. I felt very tearful and negative. The following day was completely different, I worked on my black and white prints for the club competition next week.

Many people will have their own ways of distracting themselves from problems. While this is of limited value in dealing with difficulties which need some kind of action to be taken, problems which are out of the individual's control, and especially those which will sort themselves out may often be dealt with quite effectively. The activities chosen for distraction can vary from hobbies and pastimes, social visits to or from others, or even something as simple as watching television.

Developing a range of active and passive coping strategies will not mean that the problems and setbacks of illness will become trivial, or that they can always be dealt with. It does however give the dying person an armoury with which to confront such problems, and to reduce their impact. Not only does this help in dealing with the problems, it also enhances the individual's sense of control over what is happening, helping to maintain the autonomy and sense of self so important at this time.

Summary

In getting on with living, it is inevitable that the dying person will encounter problems and setbacks. These may arise directly from the illness or its treatment, which may cause pain, incapacity and other difficulties. In addition, there will be problems which arise indirectly. These include the problems of coping with other minor illnesses, and the fears and anxieties which these may generate. On top of all these are social and personal problems, including the reactions of others and possible difficulties arising from the tension and irritability experienced by the dying person.

The solutions to such problems will, to a large extent, depend on their nature. However, some general strategies may be helpful. Recognition and anticipation of problems will often be a start in the development of solutions, which will need to be generated in the light of the dying person's own priorities and limitations; indeed, acceptance of such limitations may often be the major part of the solution.

It is possible to identify a number of additional coping strategies, both active and passive. In the former category are seeking help and support from others (both from friends and professional helpers) and the development of the skills of positive thinking. This may be helped by concentrating on progress, attending more to the good things than the bad, remembering that many problems will pass, making the most of the good times, recognizing the positive aspects of problems associated with treatment, and refusing to let problems take on a seriousness they don't merit. Other active coping strategies include the reorganization and restructuring of the physical and social environment, seeking out things like physical activity where this is helpful, and remembering to do the things that are enjoyable!

Passive strategies for coping do not necessarily attack the problem head on but provide help in dealing with it. Learning the skills of relaxation can provide an escape from the tensions and worries which arise. In much the same way, other activities such as hobbies and pastimes can provide valuable distractions from problems, in particular those which will in time sort themselves out. Whilst use of the various coping strategies described will not eliminate problems, it may certainly be possible to reduce the distress they cause, giving the dying person more and more control over what is happening to them.

Practical implications

Many of the practical implications of this chapter will have been obvious from the text. Certain issues are however worth emphasizing:

● It's inevitable that problems will arise — don't take it as a personal failure when they do. In particular, it's not necessary to feel guilty about interpersonal difficulties — they are bound to arise. Dying people, as well as those who are caring for them, are bound to feel tense and irritable at times when confronted with the worries and uncertainties involved. A common reaction when conflicts arise is to make up and then pretend they never happened. Making up is fine, but instead of forgetting the conflict, recognize the problem and try to think of what can be learned from it in terms of preventing it happening again.

- In the same way, recognize problems when they arise — often it may be helpful to predict problems. Doing so may not necessarily mean they can be avoided, but will often mean some action can be taken to prepare for and minimize their impact.

- The dying person needs to identify reasonable (though not necessarily unchanging) priorities and limitations. Dealing with problems will then be more meaningful in the context of these.

- Numerous coping strategies are available, both active and passive. Dying people, and those who are caring for them, may benefit from studying such strategies and employing them in the alleviation of problems.

- It will not be possible to solve all problems. When a problem cannot be solved, it shouldn't be taken as a personal failure. Rather, the problem should be looked at calmly, and consideration given to whether or not all the possible solutions have been tried. If not, then try something else. If all possible solutions have been tried, then the problem must be accepted as an inevitable limitation with no implications for personal failure.

6
Facing death

Although earlier chapters have concentrated not on death but on life, there is no denying that for most people with a fatal illness, concerns with death will be unavoidable. Although well-meaning friends or relatives may studiously avoid talking of death, reminders will remain all around, taking on a special significance to the dying person.

On television and radio, in newspapers and magazines, references to death and dying will abound. Characters in plays, films, and soap operas will 'die'. Documentaries, newspaper reports and magazine articles will talk of people who have died, or who are dying. To the dying person, each of these references is likely to strike a chord, throwing into one's consciousness the mysterious and usually frightening concept of death. In the same way, references to serious illness, particularly if it's to the same as the sufferer's, may well take on special significance.

In the person's direct experience, too, events will occur which have the same effect. Simply to see a funeral procession driving along the street is likely to trigger off thoughts of their own funeral in the dying person. Many dying people will be of advanced years, and will, during the course of their illness, have acquaintances, friends or relatives who die. Many serious illnesses are fairly common, and it is likely that during the course of the illness others will contract the same disease, again forcing the issue into consciousness.

In the light of all this it is probably obvious that, for most of us, attempting to avoid thinking about death at all is likely to be unsuccessful. If, as you read this book, you are in good health, try recording during a single day how many references to death, dying or serious illness you encounter. If you *are* dying, there's no need to ask you to do so; you're probably already painfully aware of how common such references are.

For many people, then, it is perhaps worth considering an alternative to avoiding the issue; confronting it on your own terms. Rather than struggle against the thoughts, only to find them bursting through whenever the struggle fails, it may be more helpful to consider quite openly the issues involved, doing so when *you* feel most able.

Perhaps the most obvious point to consider is fear of death. The notion that everyone is afraid of death is commonplace, but it is almost certainly oversimplistic. Firstly, not everyone *does* appear to be afraid of death; one lady over a hundred years old remarked that she 'prayed every night to the Lord to come and take her'. For those of many religious beliefs, and for a large number with no religious belief, death holds no fears.

Secondly, and, perhaps, more importantly for our present purposes, even amongst the massive percentage of the population for whom death is frightening, the fears are not always the same. The subject of death gives rise to many fears. Not everyone will experience all such fears, and even those who do will fear different aspects to different degrees.

Consider, for example, the fear of pain. Questions regarding how much pain may be experienced are frequently asked of doctors dealing with dying patients. The reality is that, for many people, dying *will* involve some degree of pain at some point — but, by and large, such pain will be controllable. In particular, drugs which might not be used under normal circumstances because of fears about their long-term effects can appropriately be used in the advanced stages of a fatal illness. Establishing the precise dose of such powerful drugs requires great skill on the part of the prescribing doctor. Sometimes it will become necessary to increase the dose, often with little warning, as Freda discovered:

A day which started so well ended on a rather low note. Elizabeth and I had a lovely lunch in the sun by the pond, but suddenly, as though a switch had been pulled, the pain increased.

Conversely there may well be times when painkillers can be reduced; several times during her illness Freda reduced the amount she was taking, obtaining control of pain and minimizing side-effects.

In general, pain will not be a major problem for most dying patients. Very few people in our society need die in pain, or, indeed, experience much pain through their illness. The development of powerful drugs, the use of psychological coping strategies and the availability of specialist pain clinics have all done much to bring pain associated with death under control.

Besides the fear of pain, many people may experience a rather less well-defined fear of loss. Such a fear of loss may have many aspects. To some extent, the fear may reflect the sense of exclusion which is almost inevitable; family and friends will make plans for the long-term future which, realistically, will not involve the dying person. In this sense, there *is* a loss which is concurrent with knowing that one is dying. Other losses will involve ambitions which it is clear can no longer be fulfilled. And, of course, there is the loss of family and friends, which even for those of a strong religious persuasion and belief in an afterlife is likely to be present to some degree, even if seen as only temporary.

It is notable, of course, that for many people one of the main fears of death is not for themselves but for those who are left behind. Worries about how the rest of the family will manage are commonplace and may involve not only financial and practical issues but also emotional ones. The issue may appear to be insoluble, since to pretend that the dying person will not be missed is neither practical nor reassuring. Once again, however, bringing such issues out into the open may help considerably. We saw in chapter 3 how Freda and Les discussed at length how Les would mananage after Freda's death, with such discussion going a long way to putting Freda's mind at ease.

Perhaps the central theme which runs through these and other fears relating to death, however, is the fear of the unknown. With the exception of those with strong religious or philosophical beliefs, most people will see death as involving the unknown and unknowable. Occasionally this may give rise to acute and passing anxieties. However, with growing acceptance of the situation, many dying people, particularly if they know their loved ones will manage, find themselves losing their fear of death.

During the past week I have made great progress towards accepting my situation, its uncertainty and the losses which I have sustained or will eventually sustain because of my shortened life span — particularly the disability from my stroke. As I noted from last week's entry I have spent quite a lot of time thinking, to some purpose. Some of these thoughts — the waste of time on negative thoughts — have been quite comforting and illuminating. Despite the fact that thinking has taken up quite a lot of time and energy, it represents, in my opinion, a progress towards maturity which is an essential ingredient in all human life. After all, we are all born to die, it is just that I have recently learned that I will not live as long as I had originally hoped. The bonus is that I have time to prepare myself and those around me for it . . . I realized a few days ago I was not afraid to die.

In much the same way, the dying person may come to an acceptance of separation and its effects on loved ones:

I have regained (or even just discovered) a great aura of self esteem. My loved ones will see this. I hope it will help to prepare them for the separation. The pain for them will be inevitable.

In this context, however, it is worth noting that the information that one is not afraid to die is not always welcome:

I am not so sure the communication of this, especially the thought, 'I am not afraid to die' is quite so welcome to a few others.

At first glance this might seem odd, since one might expect friends and relatives to be pleased that the fear of death has passed. There are however several possible reasons why a lack of fear may seem unwelcome. As we have seen, dying people bring to people's consciousness many of their own fears about death, and to see someone else coping successfully may increase one's own sense of inadequacy in the face of the threat. Remember, too, that separation is an important issue, and to be told that the person is not afraid to die may be interpreted as meaning that the separation is not seen as important — almost like being told, 'I don't mind that I'll never see you again.' What this means is that telling others that one is not afraid of death is not a straightforward matter, and may need to be explained in some detail. The dying person may justifiably be proud of such new-found courage in the face of death and give the statement very simply; often however it will be worth putting a little effort into explaining one's feelings in a little more detail. Doing so may also alleviate a further anxiety of friends and relatives — that in expressing no fear of death, the person is losing contact with reality. By explaining in detail how one feels, rather than simply saying that one is not afraid, one can avoid giving the suspicion that one has lost contact with reality.

Decisions about death

Acknowledgement of the fact that one's life expectancy is limited may often give rise to the need to make certain decisions about one's death. For example, although one may have little say in *when* one dies, it may be possible to determine *where* one is likely to die. For most people such a decision will involve a choice between one of perhaps three places — at home, in a hospital, or in a hospice. It is not possible to give any simple answer to the question of which of these is preferable, since much depends on the individual person and on the particular illness. It may be that for an illness requiring highly specalized treatment there is no choice, neither the home nor the hospice having the facilities available. Or there may not be a hospice within a manageable distance of loved ones. The first step to take, if you are suffering from a fatal illness and concerned about where you will die, is to discuss the matter with the doctor responsible for your treatment. The doctor will know what facilities are available locally, and enough about your illness to be able to give an idea of the practicality of each of the options. The information given to you by your doctor, in conjunction with your own assessment of the advantages and disadvantages of each of the options can then form the basis either for your final decision or for further discussion with those who are close to you.

The assessment of the advantages and disadvantages of home, hospital and hospice will inevitably depend to a great extent on the specifics of each individual's situation. Rather than give a list of such advantages and disadvantages, therefore, it is more helpful to consider some of the questions which might usefully be asked about each of the options.

For many people, dying at home will mean that loved ones can be depended upon to be close at hand at the time of death. Many people find the idea of dying alone a frightening one, and obtain great comfort from the knowledge that they are amongst their family. Obviously, this is something which, if being considered as an option, needs to be discussed with the rest of the family, since it is likely that they will need to do most of the nursing of the dying person. While some support will usually be available from the community nursing service, caring for the sick person at home will still involve some considerable effort on the part of the family. For some patients, the administration of drugs may present problems, although the development of mechanical syringe drivers which deliver controlled amounts of drug automatically may often provide a solution.

On the positive side, dying at home means that the family as a whole can make the most of their remaining time together. This may be particularly important in the later stages of an illness, where the patient may be tired a great deal of the time and only fully alert at unpredictable intervals; if such a person is in hospital, it is possible that such periods of alertness will not be those when the family are actually present. From the point of view of the family, the opportunity to care for the dying person can provide a sense of doing something to help, rather than the frustrating helplessness of standing by while others do everything. Having said that, it is natural that sometimes the demands made by the dying person will be resented, later leading to feelings of guilt. Practically everyone who has cared for a dying person has, at some time, experienced the feeling of waiting, almost impatiently, for death to occur. Those caring for the dying should be helped to understand that such feelings are natural, and do not imply any lack of love for the dying person. Nor need they result in feelings of guilt.

Dying in hospital, on the other hand, will usually involve the family in very little of the physical care of the dying person. Indeed, both the dying person and the remainder of the family may feel greater security knowing that the whole expertise of the medical, nursing and other health professions is at their disposal. For the seriously ill person, it is extremely unlikely that there will be restrictions on visiting, and, for many people, the hospital will provide an opportunity for comfort to be maintained in the presence of loved ones, without the worry that the care is too much of an imposition or that they will be unable to cope. In considering whether or not being in hospital may be preferable to dying at home, one may wish to take into account the accessibility of the hospital for family members and to obtain reassurance from ward staff that the family will be called should the person's condition deteriorate whilst the family are not there.

To many people, a hospice is seen as something in between the two options discussed above. One misleading idea about hospices needs to be corrected from the beginning — hospices are *not* simply places where people go to die. Indeed, a good many people who are admitted to hospices return to their homes after a short period of treatment. That said, there is no denying that the hospices are particularly skilled in the care of dying patients, providing both physical and emotional support. The staff of hospices will normally have had specialist training in the care of dying patients, being sensitive to both emotional and physical needs. As with hospitals, the hospice may provide a feeling of security for those who do not feel confident about being treated at home. Ideally, arrangements will be made for the hospice to be involved in treatment at an early stage — a commonly expressed fear of hospices is the anxiety prompted by thinking that admission is an indication that death is at hand. If it is admitted from an early stage that hospice admission may be a routine matter of treatment, such anxieties may be minimized. Again, as with the hospital, issues of accessibility and communication are likely to be important.

A further decision, which may have important implications for where dying would be most appropriate, concerns the donation of bodily organs. Some people find the prospect of having vital organs removed from their body after death horrific; others see it as a way of making their death a positive contribution to the well-being of others. Should your personal beliefs preclude the possibility of donating organs, the matter is settled. If, however, you are willing at least to consider the possibility, then again this is something you should discuss with your doctor. Do not make the mistake of assuming that because you are dying, your organs will be too unhealthy to be of benefit to others, or that because your eyesight is poor your corneas will be useless. It is possible, if you are willing to go ahead with donation of organs, that you will, in dying, transform the life of another human being, freeing them from the handicap of blindness, or of hours each week spent in treatment for such illnesses as kidney disease. Whether or not organ donation will be possible in your particular case will depend on the circumstances. If in doubt, ask your doctor. In doing so you may save someone else's sight or their life.

In a similar way, many individuals may have quite strong views on how they would like their own funeral arranged. Some may wish to know that the funeral will be a substantial affair, with friends and family all gathering to pay their respects; others may want only a small, private gathering. Many will be happy to leave such decisions to their next of kin. On this note it is worth remembering that many people may also have strong views on burial versus cremation. All of these matters can appropriately be discussed if they seem important to the individual. Often there is a temptation for friends and relatives to cut short such discussion, arguing that it is pessimistic or morbid. Such temptation should be resisted if possible; if the topic is important to the dying person, being prevented from discussing it will lead to frustration, not reassurance.

Intimations of death

It is verging on the inevitable that people who are aware that they are dying will experience various visions or anticipations of death itself. For Freda, as a doctor, contact with her own dying patients was obviously of great significance:

One of my first patients was X. I was saddened to find he has carcinoma of the prostate with spinal metastases. It was quite difficult to talk to him. I naively thought it should be easier to do it well, I couldn't quite work out where he was in acceptance, what he believed, what won't he believe. I didn't use the word cancer, despite the fact that he threw out the word when recalling his recent visit to Clatterbridge.

The realization that dealing with such a person was still difficult, despite her own situation, was itself distressing for Freda:

I felt it would be better to go to see (for the last time) one of my terminally ill patients . . . I found it very sad to see this lady fading and I left the house in tears. I explained to her son that I came because I had a car today. Although I was embarrassed to be seen having broken down, I was glad I'd gone to see her. Perhaps this coloured my mood for the rest of the day but it's part of my frustration that nothing ever seems to be right at the moment, however hard I try, however logical my course of action seems — in other ways, I seem trapped.

Of course, experiences such as these are peculiar to people like Freda — doctors, nurses and others dealing with the very sick. For most people, intimations of death will be very personal. As with the early response to the news that one is dying, visions of death may show their first signs in dreams:

I woke in the night in a half-dream state and I became convinced the time had come, perceptions were different. I remember a sort of ornate table with curved legs (in retrospect possibly an altar), my first cogent thought was I must tell Les, hurry, it's come. I think I said, 'The time has come, things are changing.' However, when I realized I was wrong I apologized, said 'Are you O.K.? I suppose you can get used to anything.' I awoke very disappointed, perplexed. Why should I be disappointed when I am enjoying life so much? I cried with confusion. It took all morning to get the odd, confused feeling out of my mind.

At this stage, Freda's reactions to the presence of death in her dream state were confused, leaving her unsettled. Within a few months however she was dealing with such dreams much more calmly:

One dream I had a few nights ago seems worth recording. I had a distinct sense of someone calling me over, it was from the 'other side'. I was definitely not ready, was not perturbed, gently refused. I must keep this in mind. I must continue to live positively. I know I have so many pleasurable things going for me.

And:

I must write about a rather strange experience the other night when I was gradually wakening. I had a feeling I was being called away, not by name, but to the 'other side'. I smiled inside myself, I said 'I'm not ready yet. I have a lot of living still to do.' Again, I listed in my mind the things I have to live for, first and middle and last is Les, and the girls and their future. I am aware of the value of my contibution to medicine, it will grow. I hope it becomes a bit more special than before my illness.

While, at first, such dreaming may appear to be disturbing, it may serve a useful function by enabling the dying person to become accustomed to the idea of death, to practise, as it were, facing up to death. For Freda, the early, confused responses to dreaming about death soon came to be replaced by a calm acceptance of the dreams. This may be a useful first step in learning to deal with the idea of death when awake. In particular, the dreams may well occur relatively early in the illness, when death is still actually some way off; experience of the dreams during this comparatively 'safe' period may be useful preparation for the time when physical deterioration becomes apparent and the prospect of death closer.

Physical deterioration is, of course, inevitable in many serious illnesses. We saw in chapter 5 how easy it is for increasing debilitation to be a major source of worry for the dying person, each setback, each new pain possibly heralding the imminence of death. Very often these setbacks will be overcome within a few days, allowing the fear of death to recede again:

I can report quite a lot of improvement. The pain in my right hip and the neck pain have completely disappeared today . . . also nausea and vomiting much improved.

Inevitably, however, there will come a time when the deterioration is extreme:

Events have taken a turn for the worse since the beginning of May. One day I had noticed increasing pain and spasm in the left hip as the day went on. By the time Les came to help me off the low settee up to bed, I had great difficulty in walking . . . After a few telephone calls on Saturday morning it was arranged for me to go into hospital, my admission or discharge being dependent on the results of tests.

I felt very fearful of going into hospital, having to get on and off X-ray trolleys, but eventually it was done — no fracture, the trouble is due to secondaries.

Not surprisingly, such problems were again associated with dreams about death:

I had a dream experience last night. It seemed clear there was some sort of crisis for me — something or somebody was quietly insisting, 'Please take me with you.' It seemed that I was perhaps dying but there was no physical change to make me think anything had changed.

At this stage it became clear that the problems for Freda were now acute:

A serious situation with fractured sacro-iliac joints and possibly partially collapsed bodies on 4 or 5. Not a certain situation to describe, but it has been this way all along.

Just over a fortnight later Freda died peacefully at home.

Learning from Freda's experience

Clearly, for most people, the approach of death is a frightening business, but, as we can see from Freda's experience, it is possible to learn to accept it, to reach a point where one can say, 'I am not afraid to die,' and really mean it.

To be in such a position can ease the process of deciding the important issues about one's death; where one is going to die, funeral arrangements, organ donation, and so on. However, it is important to remember at the same time that friends and relatives of the dying person may find such a viewpoint disturbing, and may need time to accept that the person is sincere in disclaiming fears. Acceptance of the dying person's feelings may be difficult, and can take quite a time. For a few people, such acceptance may never be possible.

As far as intimations of death are concerned, we have already seen that much of Freda's experience, gained through her work as a doctor, would not be shared by most people who are dying. Nevertheless, many dying people, even without such professional responsibility, can expect to meet friends, relatives or associates who are seriously ill. We saw from Freda's accounts how, even with her own professional experience and training, and her personal experience as a dying person herself, talking to other dying people wasn't easy. Perhaps, then, the first thing to learn from Freda's experience is that to be in the same position oneself doesn't make talking to other dying people any easier, and may indeed make it more difficult. The dying person who experiences such difficulties should not regard these as a sign of personal failure; they will often be inevitable.

On a more personal level, most dying people will have as Freda did, intimations of death in their dreams. We saw from Freda's accounts how, when this first started to happen, her reactions left her confused. Part of this confusion is due to the general unreality of all our dream experiences, but, perhaps more important, is the fact that early intimations of death in dreams take the person by surprise. These dreams will occur on a number of occasions, and the person who reacts to early dreams with confusion will often respond much more calmly later. It is worth remembering how frightening the unknown can be. It helps if there is someone with whom the dreams can be discussed, with a chance to describe the various reactions which occur. The way in which people react to these dreams can vary considerably; reactions like fear and anxiety are distressing, but not particularly surprising, whilst reactions like Freda's eventual disappointment may seem bewildering. The opportunity to talk to a sympathetic listener can do much to help.

Besides the psychological intimations of death, of course, we also have the various physical reminders, with physical setbacks and deteriorations being the most obvious. The kinds of 'false alarm' that Freda experienced will be shared by many people in her position. A change in the illness *may* mean that death is now close, but it will more often be something which settles again within a relatively short period of time. Changes in Freda's physical condition often led her to wonder whether or not her illness was becoming very serious, only for the problem to subside again within a few days. When it seems that the illness is taking a turn for the worse, it is often a mistake to conclude this is the beginning of the end.

Summary

Whilst it's tempting to try to avoid the subject of death, the numerous references we encounter in day-to-day life mean that this is unlikely to be practical. It may be better, therefore, to face up to the fears associated with death, dealing with them on one's own terms as and when one can. The fear of death itself will often be less significant than fears of pain, loss and separation, and, of course, fear of the unknown. Despite all this, it *is* possible to come to terms with one's own death, reaching a point where death is accepted. While acceptance may not always be well received by friends and relatives, it *does* provide comfort to the dying person, and *can* make it easier to discuss some of the practical aspects of dying and death.

Even with acceptance of the notion of death intellectually, the first intimations of death — dreams, for example — are likely to be unsettling. However, just as it is possible to adapt to conscious thoughts of death, so it is possible to adapt to its unconscious representations. Adapting to various physical setbacks may not always be so easy, since these will often be associated with other problems such as decreased mobility, increased tiredness, and so on. Yet, even with the physical problems, it will often be possible to pass through the worries and anxieties which are produced, and return to a positive attitude. Useful activity may continue surprisingly close to death. Fairly early in her illness Freda noted:

> *Have just read that Charles Douglas-Home, editor of* The Times, *died of cancer yesterday, working and dictating until ten days before his death. I think that won't be my pattern.*

Yet Freda, too, carried on working determinedly, late into her illness, still writing her diary two weeks before her death, and discussing this book right up to the last few days.

Practical implications

The prospect of death is, to some extent, frightening. In such a situation, no amount of help and advice will eliminate all anxieties for all people. Nevertheless, the points made in this chapter do suggest a number of practical implications including:

- Don't try to avoid the subject of death in the desperate hope that the dying person won't then have to think about it. There are so many things relating to death in our society anyway that the dying person will receive constant reminders of their own condition. It is much better to confront the issue of death on one's own terms than to try to avoid it and find the worries breaking through when one is least able to deal with them.

- Remember that fears relating to death can take many forms. The fear of death itself may be less worrying than fear of loss, separation, and fear of the unknown. If the dying person can discuss these fears with another person, this will do more to relieve the worries than any attempt at avoiding the subject.

- Dying people themselves may be very good at dealing with their fear of death, and accept their situation calmly. Even when this occurs, it may still be necessary to cope with the inability of others to come to terms with the dying person's acceptance. If the dying person's acceptance disturbs you, ask yourself why this could be so. If necessary, discuss it with the person concerned. Under no circumstances be dismissive or patronizing, concluding that the person is 'failing to accept reality', or 'deluding themselves'. If their acceptance raises fears about death in you, it may be that *you* can obtain reassurance from discussion.

- Don't assume that the dying person doesn't want to talk about the practical aspects of their death, or that to do so is morbid. Many people have clear ideas about where they would like to die, the donation of bodily organs, the relative merits of burial and cremation, and so on. To know that the next of kin are aware of their wishes can go a long way in reducing anxiety associated with dying.

- Be prepared to experience intimations of death in a variety of forms, especially in dreams. Early reactions to such intimations may be disturbing, or confusing, but, as with conscious thoughts of death, acceptance does occur. When there are advances in one's illness, it's easy to think, 'This is it, the time has come.' However, many diseases have periods of stability interspersed with definite changes. Try to remember that setbacks aren't always permanent, that they often pass. Even a change for the worse which isn't passing still doesn't mean that death is imminent. Thinking positively when these setbacks occur will reduce the fears and anxieties.

- Don't give up the things you like doing without a fight. Many people continue with activities that are important to them to within days of their death. A dying person doesn't have to be a helpless person.

7
The future: Society and death

It should be clear from the preceding chapters that there is much to be said for 'opening up' the topic of death in society. Most of us will at some time find ourselves close to others who are dying, and all of us will have to confront the knowledge of our own impending deaths, whether from illness or old age. We saw in chapter 1 how the topic of death is becoming more accessible and acceptable, with scientific studies, books and articles discussing aspects of death and dying being more widely published. There remains, however, considerable scope for the extension of such accessibility to a number of areas in society.

Education

The commonplace notion that children should somehow be 'protected' from death involves a number of problems. Obviously, for a number of children, such protection is impossible. A parent, sibling, or other close member of the family may die. A best friend may die, from illness or accident. Some children are themselves dying. The child confronted with such events is not helped by the philosophy of 'protection'. Indeed such a philosophy serves only to increase the child's feeling of isolation. Instead of being able to share feelings with other children, the child learns that the subject is taboo, that other children have been encouraged to avoid the issue. In such a situation, the most likely outcomes are either isolation, since no other child can do anything to help, or fear and confusion as other children attempt to share from a position of ignorance and superstition.

It can be argued that the costs to the minority of children who are personally concerned is offset by the benefits to the majority who are not. According to this argument, it is better to leave the minority in distress than to frighten or upset the majority by raising such issues. This might have some force if children had no concept of death, but this is not the case. Children *do* have thoughts, feelings and beliefs about death, from quite an early age. If they see that adults avoid the topic, this is much more likely to be frightening than a calm, reasoned discussion. Children's fears about death will not be alleviated if they sense that such fears have to be kept secret and cannot be talked about. However, to talk about the fears in a sensible way with an adult who approaches the topic calmly can provide considerable reassurance. In many cases there may be much to be said for incorporating teaching about death and dying into the regular school curriculum. This could have both academic and personal elements. The academic content could take into account the increasing scientific knowledge about the experience of dying and the various concepts of dying of different religions and philosophies. The personal could provide opportunity to discuss personal opinions, feelings, thoughts and speculations about death.

Later in the educational system, of course, this might seem to be particularly crucial — as in the teaching and training of doctors, nurses, psychologists, social workers and others working with the dying. At the same time, it is important to remember that it is not practical simply to leave the topic to such professional groups and to ignore the needs of the general public. It is, after all, important that everyone who is confronted with problems of death and dying receives some preparation. Nevertheless, it is obvious that, if attitudes and practices are to change, those who are professionally involved are likely to be in the forefront.

The caring professions

The majority of professionals involved in caring for the dying receive inadequate preparation for their role. There is a pressing need for careful training of relevant professional groups in dealing with issues of death. The continuing education of professional groups should include seminars, workshops and courses at periodic intervals during their working lives where they can discuss the issues that arise with other concerned people.

The issues are not, however, simply ones of training. One of the more frustrating experiences for those attempting to improve the provision of care for the dying is the frequency with which professional groups squabble childishly about who is responsible.

Some argue that only the medical profession should break the news to patients, since they are the only ones with the detailed knowledge of the illness. Others argue that a detailed knowledge of the patient is at least as important as knowledge of the illness, and that the nurse is more likely to have such knowledge. Or it may be argued that psychologists are in the best position, with their expert knowledge of how fears and anxieties arise and what can be done about them. Social workers may appear to be the best choice, with their knowledge of sources of support, help for the bereaved and so forth. For those with a spiritual perspective, it might appear that a chaplain would be the person of choice.

The reality is that such interprofessional squabbling masks the important issues. None of the characteristics referred to is anything like as important as the need for tact, sensitivity and a willingness to listen and help – and these are not the prerogative of any professional group. Much will depend on the particular relationship between the patient and the individual members of the team caring for them. Often the patient will choose who should tell them by choosing who to ask. Where special skills are required, medical, psychological, social or spiritual, they can always be sought from the appropiate sources. Often the need for this information can be anticipated and the information obtained in advance.

It is a sobering observation that most hospitals don't have an operational policy with respect to informing and caring for dying patients. Calls for such a policy are usually met with resistance, and a reminder that rigid policies are inappropriate for dealing with the individualities of patients. However, the lack of a policy may lead to much greater inflexibility, with the whims or unjustified personal opinions of powerful individuals taking the place of reasoned discussion. In discussing these issues at meetings and conferences, for example, it is commonplace for hospital nurses to state that they are not allowed to answer when patients ask, 'Do I have cancer?' or, 'Am I dying?' because is has been decreed that only the doctor can decide whether and how to answer such a question. Yet often asking such a question can involve the patient concerned in plucking up considerable courage; to be fobbed off with evasion may discourage them from ever asking the question again (and incidentally may lead the less sophisticated and more smug doctor to conclude that since the question wasn't repeated, that the patient 'didn't really want to know'). However, it is likely that not only do patients choose to ask at a time when they feel most ready to take the news, they are also likely to ask the person from whom they would most like to hear it. Arbitrary rules about who should tell can have the effect of depriving the patient of the right to hear at a chosen time from a preferred source.

A more realistic and considerate policy would involve discussion between all members of a care team when the seriousness of a diagnosis is first suspected. At this point, the team, with all relevant disciplines represented, can consider whether or not there is good reason for withholding information from the patient, and, if not, when and how the patient should be told and by whom. Where there is disagreement, the reasons for the disagreement should be made explicit. Disagreement may result from lack of information, in which case the information can be sought out, or from differences in opinion, in which case the reasons for the opinions can be explored, opinions based on rational consideration being distinguished from opinions based on prejudice or superstition. If necessary, outside expertise should be called upon to clarify differences of opinion and to help resolve disagreements.

The expertise of professionals can also often be put to good use in the provision and development of support groups for dying people and those who care for them. Such support groups are becoming increasingly common, with several groups already existing in Britain, the United States and other countries. Some such groups are organized nationally, others locally. (We give some addresses at the end of the book.) Local organizations can be found through Citizen's Advice Bureaux, local libraries, etc.

Personal changes

Besides broader social changes, our own attitudes to death may need careful scrutiny. If talking about death embarrasses us, we should not be surprised if our interactions with dying people are awkward, or that talking about our own death makes us uncomfortable. Talking about death can make us less embarrassed. With thought, this can also tell us more about ourselves and the people we love. Try, for example, the following exercise. Think of a number of illnesses, not all necessarily serious. You may for example consider heart disease, stroke, lung cancer, multiple sclerosis, stomach cancer — or any other disease that occurs to you. Write them on a piece of paper, then number them in order of how distressed you would be if you had the disease diagnosed. If for example you would be most distressed by lung cancer, then by heart disease, these would be numbered one and two. Carry on until you reach the end of the list — you may find it difficult to choose between some of them and end up giving them the same number. Repeat the numbering for how you think your spouse, partner or other close loved ones would feel. Then make a second list of the factors that influence your decisions — whether the disease is life-threatening, disfiguring, involves dependency on others, what treatment would be involved and so on, numbering these in order of which factors are most important for you and your partner. If your partner also numbers the same lists, you may be surprised at how badly you predict each other's order. Having done all this, you are likely to learn a lot from discussing each other's conclusions. In a similar way, you can explore your own and other people's feelings about being informed about serious illness, about funerals, and so on. Above all, perhaps, we need to rid ourselves of the superstitious beliefs that if we talk about death we'll somehow bring it upon ourselves, or that if we don't talk about it, it won't happen.

In addition, of course, we need to look carefully at the messages we give our children about the topic of death. Such messages may be both explicit and implicit. If we tell our children not to be morbid when they ask about death, or if we avoid the subject, they will soon learn not to mention it — and thus lose the opportunity to share and relieve any fears or anxieties they may have. Carefully examine your motives before preventing children from attending a funeral, or keeping them away from a dying person, or not telling them that a friend or relative is dying. Ask yourself how you feel about your children seeing you grieving. If we are afraid of our childreen seeing us upset, or in tears, what are we pretending to be to our children? Few, if any, children have the need to believe that their parents are immune from hurt, sorrow or grief, indeed there may often be a greater danger that the child sees the parent who hides grief following a loss as uncaring, cold or distant.

Changes in patterns of dying: The problems of AIDS

It is worth highlighting the fact that recent years have raised the spectre of many more deaths, slow and distressing, from the disease AIDS. It is too soon to say how many people will die from AIDS, and to make any general statements about how those with the disease will react to it. Certainly we can expect the reactions of those with AIDS to have much in common with those of other

dying people — denial, anger, bargaining, depression and acceptance may all be present. In addition, however, the nature of the
disease and its mode of transmission makes it likely that other
problems, too, will arise. Amongst the relevant factors we may
note:

- *The age group concerned* Unlike most other diseases which
  account for a large number of deaths, AIDS strikes at a
  relatively young age. This may have many consequences,
  including a sense of injustice (both to the victim and other others)
  that death should come to one so young, that there is so little
  opportunity to prepare and so on. On a broad scale, of course,
  an epidemic of substantial proportions could have major implications for the age distribution of our society.

- *How it is spread* Rightly or wrongly, AIDS, unlike most other
  fatal illnesses, has a number of moral connotations attached to
  it. The AIDS victim is likely to have to cope with the shame and
  remorse associated with having acquired the disease.

- *The guilt involved* Although, as we have seen, many dying
  people may feel guilty about their illness, this is likely to be
  particularly problematic for the AIDS victim. Moreover, since
  the behaviour concerned is likely to be one censured by
  society, the likelihood of guilt is further increased.

- *Social isolation* Unlike most fatal diseases, AIDS is conta-
  gious. Already high-risk individuals are finding themselves
  isolated from friends who no longer wish to see them because
  of the fear of AIDS. Among those who do have the virus, not
  only is fear likely to lead to the loss of support of some friends,
  but also to limitations on the amount of support given by
  others; as one AIDS victim, constantly handled in hospital
  through rubber gloves remarked, 'Will I never be held again?'

- *Anger* The problem of isolation is compounded by the fact
  that, for many sufferers, there will be anger directed at the
  sexual partner who has, unwittingly, passed on the disease.
  Thus the loved one who might have been turned to at such a
  time may be regarded with at best ambivalence and at worst
  hostility.

- *Hope* As things stand at the moment there is little basis for
  any hope on the part of AIDS sufferers. Although survival
  times vary, all are relatively short (a year is a long time for a
  person with full-blown AIDS to live) and the time itself is likely

to be extremely distressing with weakness, disfigurement and additional anxieties. No-one has ever been cured of AIDS and the treatments which have so far been devised may prolong life, but do little if anything to add to its quality.

Of course, not all sufferers experience all the difficulties and feelings described above. For many, the discovery that they have the virus has led to a number of positive outcomes, ranging from the determination to campaign on behalf of other sufferers to improvements in close relationships. Nevertheless, there is every possibility that the coming years will see a phenomenal number of AIDS deaths. If we are to help these victims, we must be prepared for every eventuality.

Summary

There are many reasons for believing that regarding death as a taboo subject has been, at least to some extent, counter-productive. Hopefully, the coming years will see death becoming not only more acceptable as a topic of conversation, but also something with which people feel familiar and at ease. The 'opening up' of the subject of death may occur in a number of ways. Young people should be allowed to learn about death, both through the educational system and through experience of the deaths of pets, relatives and others. More importantly, perhaps, when such experiences occur, young people will feel able to discuss their thoughts, feelings and beliefs with others. At a later stage of education, teaching about death and dying should form an important part in the training of the professionals involved in the area.

Associated with the teaching and training of professionals is the development of explicit policies by those organizations concerned with the care of the dying. Such policies need not interfere with the need to treat patients as individuals; flexibility can be built into policies about the care of the dying just as it can be built into policies about the prescription of restricted drugs, or even on the visiting of patients. Without such policies there is a constant risk that procedures will be decided not on the basis of informed knowledge but rather on the basis of the opinions and prejudices of powerful individuals. In this respect, it should be noted that decisions regarding the care of the dying requires the involvement of a number of disciplines. No one professional group is likely to have all the knowledge and skills necessary for dealing with such issues. If at all possible, the knowledge and skills of interdisciplinary teams should be made available to the friends and relatives of the dying. Often such information will be obtained from self-help and support groups.

At a personal level, also, we can make efforts to feel more at ease with the subject of death, and to be sure that we are aware not only of our own feelings but also those of our loved ones. In particular, we can pay attention to the messages about dying that children pick up from our responses, and help them to learn that dying is a natural part of living.

Finally, we all need to give consideration to the impact of AIDS on society. In some countries, AIDS is already at epidemic level, and in the years to come the same may apply to our own society. Whilst the person dying of AIDS is likely to share many of the experiences of other dying people, there is the risk that the specific features of the disease and its transmission will lead to other problems including a reaction to the age of the victim, shame, guilt, isolation, anger towards one's partner and the lack of any real reason for hope. Such problems make it even more important that our knowledge of the experience of dying improves, along with our ability to be of assistance.

Practical implications

Given that we should become more open about the subject of death, it is appropriate to ask what we can actually do to facilitate such openness. No doubt different readers may have their own ideas. We might like to consider the following:

- If you are at all involved in education, give careful thought to any opportunities to introduce the topic into the classrooms. Possibilities might include inviting the clergy, the medical profession and others to talk to pupils about their concepts of death. If you're worried about raising anxieties unnecessarily, discussing similar issues when prompted by relevant stories in the news can be an easy and appropriate way of raising the subject. As members of parent-teacher associations or boards of governors it may be possible to make your opinions known about the desirability of including such topics into the curriculum.

- In a similar way, if you are involved in the care of the dying or in the training of carers, you may be able to campaign for more time to be given to both teaching the subject and the opportunity to resolve personal anxieties and difficulties of people caring for the dying and those close to them.

- Those involved in the care of the dying can also make efforts to make the subject more open. Medical consultants, managers and others with influence in the health service can raise the issues within their organization, seeking out expert guidance and considering the development of explicit policies with respect to the problems involved. In this context, one should beware of assuming that any one professional group has particular expertise, or qualifies as the ultimate arbiter of disagreement. In the area of dying there are few, if any, experts, and those who do exist are certainly not restricted to any single profession.

- If you are dying, or caring for the dying, consider making contact with the various support and self-help groups which exist. If possible, try not only to benefit from such groups, but also to be of help. Such help may range from sharing experiences to giving time to fund-raising and publicizing activities.

- Try to become more at ease with the subject of death. Talk about it with others, and, if this is awkward or embarrassing, talk about the awkwardness and the embarrassment. Share your thoughts, feelings, anxieties and opinions with loved ones — and listen to theirs. Consider carefully how your attitudes to death may be picked up by your children.

- Remember that if dying is difficult, it may be especially so for the AIDS sufferer. These people do not need blame — they will already have blamed themselves enough. Neither do they need to be avoided, for they will already feel cut off from others. When someone you know has AIDS, try to fight your own fears, anxieties or prejudices in order to give the love and support which they need.

- Finally, remember that a book like this must to some extent contain a number of over-generalizations. Do not assume that because we have highlighted things which may happen, or may be important, that these *will* happen or *will* be important. This book should not be seen as a framework into which your own or other people's experience should be forced; rather it is a first step towards understanding your own, and other people's experience. We hope you have found it helpful.

Useful organizations

When writing to any of the organizations listed below, please ensure that you include a stamped addressed envelope for your reply, as all of them are run on limited funds.

The Association of Carers can offer support and advice to those looking after relatives with any illness. They can also provide information on welfare rights and counselling. There is a network of local groups as well. Contact them at 21–23 New Road, Chatham, Kent ME4 4QJ. Tel. 0634 813981.

BACUP (British Association of Cancer United Patients) was established by Vicky Clement Jones, a doctor who had, and eventually died from, cancer. BACUP provides help and support for people with cancer and those caring for them. They can give information and advice on all aspects of cancer and can be contacted at 121–123 Charterhouse Street, London EC1M 6AA. Tel. 01 608 1661.

The British Association for Counselling will refer people to local counsellors, and can put people in touch with counsellors experienced in helping people with cancer or other terminal illnesses. Contact them at 37a Sheep Street, Rugby, Warwickshire CV27 2BX. Tel. 0788 78328/9.

Body Positive is a helpline for people who have been diagnosed as being HIV-1 positive (carrying the virus which can lead to AIDS). The number is 01 373 9124, and it is open 7 – 10 every day.

Cancerlink A support and information service for people with cancer and a resource for over 300 cancer support and self-help groups. They also distribute a range of information booklets on various forms and aspects of cancer and caring for the dying, and a video on breast cancer. They can be contacted at 17 Brittannia Street, London WC1. Tel. 01 833 2451.

The Chest, Heart and Stroke Association can provide small grants for people suffering from the illnesses that fall under their umbrella. You will need to go through a social worker for this. They can also give help and advice to anyone who contacts them. Their address is Tavistock House North, Tavistock Square, London WC1H 9JE. Tel. 01 387 3012.

The Compassionate Friends is an organization run by bereaved parents to help other parents in the same position. Contact them at 6 Denmark Street, Bristol, BS1 5DQ. Tel. 0272 292778.

CRUSE is a national organization which offers counselling to all the bereaved to help with emotional difficulties and practical advice. There is a national network of local branches, and their head office is at 126 Sheen Road, Richmond, Surrey TW9 1UR. Tel. 01 940 4818/9047.

Help the Hospices Provides support for professionals and research and training. Contact them at BMA House, Tavistock Square, London WC1H 9JP.

The Hospice Information Service will provide a Directory of Services including in-patient units, home care support teams and hospital support teams in the UK and Eire. Their address is St Christopher's Hospice, Lawrie Park Road, Sydenham, London SE26 6DZ. Tel. 01 778 1240/9252.

The Intractable Pain Society will provide the addresses of Pain Relief Clinics thoughout the country. Write to them at Association of Anaesthetists of Great Britain and Ireland, 9 Bedford Square, London WC1B 3RA. Tel. 01 686 8808.

The Lisa Sainsbury Foundation provides information and education service to support professional people who care of the dying, especially nurses. Their address is 8-10 Crown Hill, Croydon, CR0 1RY. Tel. 01 686 8808.

The Marie Curie Memorial Foundation runs hospices and a home nursing service for people with cancer. Contact them at 28 Belgrave Square, London SW1X 8QG. Tel. 01 235 3325. They can also be contacted through the Community Nursing Officer of your Local Area Health Authority.

The Sue Ryder Foundation runs the Sue Ryder Homes for the

continuing care of the seriously ill. For further details write to the foundation at Cavendish, Sudbury, Suffolk CO10 8AY. Tel. 0787 280252.

The Terrence Higgins Trust runs a Helpline to offer support, advice and information for people with AIDS, their partners, relatives and friends. The number is 01 242 1010, and the lines are open 3–10 pm every day.

Some further reading

Personal accounts

A number of writers have produced personal accounts of either serious illness or the experience of dying. A few examples are:

Twelve Weeks in Spring by June Callwood, published by Lester and Orpen Dennys, Toronto, Canada 1986. Half of the royalties from this book are donated to Casey House, a Canadian Hospice.
An Autumn Life by Ethel Helman, published by Faber and Faber, London, 1986.
A Reckoning by May Sarton, published by the Women's Press, London 1984; first published by W.W. Norton, New York, U.S.A., 1978.
Secret Flowers: Mourning and the adaption to loss by Mary Jones, published by the Women's Press, London, 1988.

All of the above, and similar books commonly available, are fairly easy to read at the same time as being very moving. Whilst not specifically aimed at a professional audience, most professionals would still benefit considerably from reading them.

Books written by professionals working in the field

Recent years have seen a considerable growth in the number of books written by doctors, nurses and others working with the dying. Inevitably it is only possible to list a small number here; there are many other excellent works which we are unable to include.

The Dying Patient: A supportive approach by Rita E. Caughill, published by Little Brown and Company, Boston, U.S.A., 1976.

Dying at Home by Harriet Copperman, published by John Wiley and Sons, Chichester, England, 1983.

Dying by John Hinton, published by Penguin Books, Harmondsworth, Middlesex, England, 1967.

On Death and Dying by Elisabeth Kubler-Ross, published by Tavistock, London, England, 1970.

Death: the final stage of growth by Elisabeth Kubler-Ross, published by Simon and Schuster, New York, U.S.A., 1975.

On Children and Death by Elisabeth Kubler-Ross, published by MacMillan Publishing Company, New York, 1983.

The Dying Patient by Ronald R. Raven, published by Pitman Medical, Tunbridge Wells, Kent, 1975.

Loss and Grief: Psychological management in medical practice edited by Bernard Schoenberg, Arthur C. Carr, David Peretz and Austin Kutscher, published by Columbia University Press, New York, U.S.A., 1970.

The Facts of Death: A complete guide for being prepared by Michael A. Simpson, published by Prentice Hall, Englewood Cliffs, New Jersey, U.S.A., 1979.

Whilst most of these are written for professionals, the lay reader is still likely to find their reading worthwhile. These books are unlikely to be in most High Street bookshops or libraries, but can usually be obtained fairly quickly; talk to your bookseller or librarian. A word of warning — some of the books, particularly the American ones, can be quite expensive, so it may be worth checking this out before ordering!

Index